SONNY LISTON
The Champ Nobody Wanted

by
A.S. "Doc" Young

FOREWORD

In these times of stress, when the cry, "boxing should be abolished," is heard in various corners of the land, Charles (Sonny) Liston looms up as the best testimonial the sport has had in ages. Liston, the world's heavyweight champion, proves beyond doubt that boxing can be worthwhile. With the aid of boxing, Sonny has boot strapped himself up from the original poverty and squalor of an Arkansas sharecropper's farm to international acclaim, a 21-room mansion in Chicago, riches of which he dared not dream ten years ago. With the aid of boxing, Sonny has been enabled to escape the shackles of a dreary life that centered, in his teens and thereafter for several years, on unfortunate encounters with the law.

This book, an unauthorized biography, traces the life of Sonny Liston from his birth in January or May, 1932, 1933, or 1934—the record is obscure—through the night of September 25, 1962, when he startled the world of boxing by knocking out Floyd Patterson in 2:06 of the first round of their title bout in Chicago's Comiskey Park. When Liston entered the ring that night, he was the most "unwanted" challenger since Jack Johnson. He was the object of boos and derision. But, his superior strength and power could not be contained by the favoritism accorded Patterson, nor by Floyd's feeble efforts at fighting.

In this book, the author has striven for objectivity, to dig through the mounds of controversy built up by the angle of evil that once permeated Liston's career, thereby to leave him revealed as he actually is. This, be it known, is no attempt at crucifixion, nor of judgment. And nothing pleases the author more than the observation that, since he defeated Patterson, Liston has been one of the great champions of our times, making himself available to the public at fights the nation over, supporting charities, giving of his time to slum kids who need all the inspiration they can get.

Many sources have contributed to the writing of this book. Research has been as extensive as humanly possible within the framework of time. The author wishes to acknowledge the contributions of the following: Mrs. Helen Liston, mother of Sonny; Tony Anderson, an early trainer in St. Louis; Monroe Harrison, an early trainer and part-manager; Frank Mitchell, St. Louis newspaper publisher, who was his first manager; the staff of the research library of Johnson Publishing Company; members of the sports staff of the St. Louis Globe-Democrat, who graciously permitted research of their files; Malcolm Poindexter, a Philadelphia writer who conducted numerous interviews of Liston's friends, acquaintances and associates in Philadelphia; and Ben Bentley, Chicago publicist. The author is also indebted for important quotes to nationally known writers Robert L. Burnes, Dick Young, Charles Chamberlain, Milton Gross, Ray Brennan, Wendell Smith, Ted Poston, Gene Courtney, George Puscas, Pete Hamill, Dan Parker, Red Smith, Thomas C. Link, and to Sen. Estes Kefauver.

And, finally, most sincere thanks to Mrs. Ariel Strong of the Johnson Publishing Company staff for her invaluable, dedicated assistance.

A. S. "DOC" YOUNG
February 13, 1963

TABLE OF CONTENTS

"The guy I like most is Joe Louis. In the ball park where Louis won the title, I am going to make it, too, as quick as I can."

—Sonny Liston, in Ring magazine, August, 1962.

"On the night he faces Patterson, Liston will move out of his corner dead set on annihilation, his eyes filled with evil, his powerful legs conditioned by girlish rope-skipping, his meanness fortified by raw meat. Ringside will be no place for the squeamish, the moralistic or the faint of heart. And in the ring it will take all of the champion's courage and skill to survive."
—Marsh Smith, writing in the February 23, 1962, issue of *Life* magazine.

CHAPTER I

When Charles (Sonny) Liston climbed into the boxing ring in Chicago's Comiskey Park to challenge Floyd Patterson for the heavyweight championship of the world, he was greeted by a raucous barrage of boos. The majority of the 18,894 paying customers, presumably present to witness a sporting event, booed Liston for one reason only: he was one of the unfortunates, an ex-convict; a self-admitted juvenile robber, an alleged cop beater, an accused perjurer. The fact that he was, nevertheless, a free man, one who had paid his debt to society, did nothing to soften the public's attitude. These people had paid their money (for the record, many of the four thousand [free ticket holders] booed too!). They held this prejudice. They presumed that it was their right to boo—and they did, like a convention of foghorn blowers.

In pre-fight publicity, in the voluminous stories and features written about this title bout, Liston had been cast irrevocably in the role of *Evil*. He had been cast in this role by strangers, who seemed never to have had so much fun as they had while labeling him "the bad boy of boxing," because of his personal difficulties with the law. Floyd Patterson, ironically a reformed juvenile delinquent himself, was cast as the unassailable character, *Good*. Liston, whose record of wrongdoing was more recent and more adult, was the Villain of this episode. Patterson was assigned the halo of Mr. Clean.

Under the circumstances, the booing was predictable, although the quality of sportsmanship of the indulgers was dubious. The booing was also unmistakable evidence of considerable hypocrisy among the fans themselves. For they, the fans, had established Liston as a solid betting favorite to win the fight and, of course, the title. They had, in other words, bet their money on *Evil*. Now, they were paying lip-service to *Good*.

In one of those monumental quirks that make sport and life interesting, in this showdown between these powerful forces, it was Liston, the portrayer of *Evil*, who exemplified one of the greatest attributes of *Good* . . .

Truth!

Hundreds of times during the two years or more that he had relentlessly chased the artfully dodging champion in quest of a title shot, Liston had told what he believed to be the absolute truth, which was the absolute truth. He said he would win—big and quick—if the two of them ever met in a fight, anywhere. After Comiskey Park, home of the American League baseball White Sox, had been selected as the site of the championship bout, Liston said he would "make it too, as quick as I can" in the same place where, on June 22, 1937, Joe Louis knocked out James J. Braddock in the eighth round to become the world's heavyweight champion. Liston said repeatedly, and specifically, that a fight between him and Patterson would end within five rounds, in a knockout, and that he would emerge victorious. He never vacillated, he never deviated, from this prediction.

In a candid moment during the Spring of 1962, Liston calmly accepted the unfavorable personal role assigned to him and, in a quiet voice that rang with the kind of self-confidence which is often described as being admirable, he threw down this manly, if not Emily Post type, challenge:

"I'm the bad guy. Okay, peoples want to think that, let them. Only—bad guys are supposed to lose. I change that. I win."

2

History records this fact: Sonny Liston kept his word, to the last letter and period. If anything, he improved on his promise. Doing this, he left the local, in-person audience and millions of fans watching theatre television and hearing the fight via radio and reading about it the next day in newspapers in a state of shock and confusion. If Patterson was *Good*, then *Good* was left in shambles.

Even while they collected the winning money that Evil had brought them, many pro-Liston bettors who were, simultaneously, pro-Patterson cheerleaders, refused to accept the fact—or, accepting it, did so grudgingly and reluctantly—that Liston was now heavyweight champion of the world. In their mad dash to rationalization, some claimed "it was a fix," others said Patterson "was terrified" (which, in truth, on comparing his qualifications to Liston's, he should have been!), and still others attempted to salve their disappointment, their wrong guesses, their mismatched wagers, by poking fun at their fallen hero. One member of the latter clan suggested that Patterson should forget all about the contracted rematch and "ask them to send the money and the knockout by mail." With Liston ruling the heavyweight division, the division which rules boxing traditionally, more than a few observers (suddenly viewing pugilism as a Sunday afternoon tea-party or a Sunday School class from which little boys draw spiritual strength) said the sport was suffering its death-rattles. One or two, if not ten or twelve, compared Liston to Jack Johnson, as if Jack Johnson had something to do with it; his major "crime," perhaps his only crime, having been the violation of the American Caste System in his relationships with white women, contracted after a couple of Negro women had inflicted upon him a broken heart.

At work throughout this "post-mortem" was a basic inconsistency which had never ceased to operate since Sonny Liston was born into an impoverished family of Arkansas sharecroppers thirty years earlier. This basic inconsistency was compounded with a lot of other inconsistencies . . . in the telling of his birth, of his flight from Arkansas, of his troubles with the law, of his beginnings in boxing, of his managerial associations—inconsistencies, inconsistencies, inconsistencies! except on the occasions when Liston stepped into the ring. Except when he faced Floyd Patterson for the world's heavyweight championship. And here was another: at the end of the

3

evening of September 25, 1962—while the conquered and embarrassed Patterson raced toward New York seclusion, tragi-comically attired in a stage-actor's mustache and beard—it was Liston, creator of a fine standard of efficiency for heavyweight title fighters, who was forced to beg the public for mercy.

"If the public allows me the chance to let bygones be bygones, I'll be a worthy champ," he said seriously, as he sat in his dressing room at Comiskey Park. "If they'll accept me, I'll prove it to them."

An inquirer wanted to know if Liston had said anything to Patterson after the knockout. "Yes," Liston replied, proving again the age-old contention that there is some good in everyone, "I thanked him for giving me the chance. Then I told him, 'I'll be as much of a man toward you as you were to me. And you were a heck of a good man.'"

There was much, much more to all the pre-fight planning, problems, and publicity and the "post-mortems" than there was to the bout itself. The bout, as the world knows, was simply a matter of a superior fighter stepping out of his corner at the first bell and annihilating an out-classed opponent in the shortest possible time. Liston knocked out Patterson in 2:06 of the first round, and this was the third fastest knockout in the history of heavyweight title fighting. In 1908, at Dublin, champion Tommy Burns kayoed Irish Jem Roche in 1:28 (one minute, twenty-eight seconds). In their rematch on June 22, 1938, Joe Louis knocked out Max Schmeling in 2:04 of the first round.

The result was hardly more, or different, from what should have been expected. Liston was the larger man (214 pounds to 189 pounds), the vastly stronger man (certainly one of the strongest heavyweights who ever lived, if not the strongest); he carried into the ring a huge advantage in reach, he was deceptively fast, unusually so for a man of his size; he had fought more rugged opponents and had beaten virtually all of them with ease. Patterson meanwhile was concentrating much of his activity on mediocrities, several of whom knocked him down. Liston's very birth, upbringing, and lifelong battle for survival as a human being in a rough-tough asphalt jungle, established him logically as the favorite to win a contest in a sport which was keyed, as it always has been, to mayhem. Rightly or wrongly, Liston had expressed himself as believing, at various stages of his life, that the world was against him; that he had to take on the whole world in a fight for survival. In essence, the title fight preserved that illusion, or disillusion. He was the favorite; but he wasn't the favorite. He said he would win, ANYWAY. He won, ANYWAY!

The first minute of the fight did not clearly foretell the outcome. Fact is, the outcome was never foretold to anyone who was sitting more than a few feet from the ring on this damp, chilly night.

During the opening exchange between the fighters, Liston missed with a jab and Patterson missed with a hook. Liston, who had remained all but inactive while chasing Patterson for the title bout itself, missed with more than a few seemingly aimless punches, during the early going. Patterson, who apparently brought no battle plan with him, believed (as he said later) that Liston would start slowly, that the early moments would be devoted to the usual bit of feeling-out of opponents. Except for the aforementioned left hook which sped past Liston's ear, Patterson never once attempted to dominate the fight, champion though he was. He threw one of his patented, leaping rights, but never showed his trumpeted "speed" to any advantage. His costliest mistake was an attempt to fight Liston inside; and it was here, although Liston's thudding body punches weren't paid the post-fight tributes they deserved, that Patterson was set up for the eventual knockout. Patterson failed miserably in his attempts to tie up Liston in the clinches.

When Patterson managed to tie up one of Liston's arms, Sonny belted Floyd's body with the other. Liston moved Patterson around with the ease of a full-grown man handling a little boy, which is the way Tony Anderson, an early Liston trainer in St. Louis, later described the two fighters.

Patterson managed to escape many of Liston's errant punches in the first minute by assuming a deep crouch, by bobbing and weaving. But in about one minute, Liston hit Patterson a blow to the kidney. Patterson's legs wobbled. Liston soon began to find the range of Patterson's head, landing with hooks.

Liston clouted Patterson with an uppercut *that lifted Patterson from the floor.* Patterson fell into a clinch.

Liston landed two left hooks. Patterson grabbed the top strand of the ropes.

The knockout was fashioned from this barrage:

Two rights to the head, two lefts to the head, then a smashing left to the head that draped Patterson over the ropes, a grazing overhand right to the head and, finally, a solid left hook from below that partially lifted Patterson's torso.

Patterson went down. Referee Frank Sikora picked up the timekeeper's count. Patterson was still down when Sikora tolled the finishing "ten." Patterson was groggy when he arose. It appeared that Patterson was saved from buckling again by the referee's arms.

That was it. A simple fight. An easy knockout. A new champion.

As usual, Patterson, a soft-spoken man who was the youngest fighter ever to win the heavyweight title as well as the first to lose it and regain it, had quite a lot to say. The most significant thing he said after Liston knocked him out was this:

"Possibly this victory will give Liston a chance to see himself. I think he's a great fighter, but people won't accept him because he's not a great man. But he can be a good man if he gets the chance to show what's within him. I think it will surprise a lot of people. If they'd only believe Liston was any kind of human being."

During the tedious pre-fight period, when it seemed that Liston would have to pay a quart of blood for every step made toward his goal, there was some discussion over prospective referees for the title match. Liston said he'd be satisfied with any referee "as long as he can count to ten."

After the fight, Liston was asked if Patterson had hurt him at any time.

"Only once," Sonny said. "That was when the man said 'nine' and it looked like he might get up before 'ten.' "

"Did you see it?"
"I didn't see anything."
"What about you?"
"Where?"
"A hook to the body."
"No—it was the head."
"What head? . . ."
—Snatches of conversation by a group of fellows who were talking about the fight, at Comiskey Park, a half-hour after it ended.

CHAPTER II

The boos for Sonny Liston were stifled by the sudden ending of the fight. The applause for Floyd Patterson was silenced by his inglorious defeat. "It was sad to see," said former champion James J. Braddock. "An amateur in there with a pro. A champion, too!—you expect more from somebody like that."

The people present were too thoroughly bewildered by Liston's easy conquest to tender to him, now, the tribute he'd earned. But, alas, inside the ring . . . ROUSING CHEERS!

In actuality, the spectators were caught up in a mystery. They were so unprepared for Liston's rapid vicious attack that few of them saw, or knew, what had happened. Like Patterson, they weren't geared to Liston's fast start.

Most of the featured and bit players in this fistic drama were, themselves, unsure of the sequence of punches that flattened Patterson; they were unsure any punches at all had been thrown. Any testimony they might have made in court later would have been strictly circumstantial, or pure hearsay. Liston demolished his foe with such tremendous finesse that, in the outer regions of the ball park, there was some doubt that the fight had even started. There were paying customers who had merely turned around to say "hello" to friends and had missed, in that flash, all the vital action. "I paid a hundred dollars for a seat," said one disgusted would-be ringsider. "But I didn't even get to my seat, much less see a fight!"

Cus D'Amato was Floyd Patterson's manager. Buster Watson was another Patterson aide. They were as close to the action as anybody, excepting Referee Sikora. But as Patterson fell to the canvas, on his way to the knock-out count, D'Amato asked Watson: "What did he get hit with?'"

"I don't know," Watson replied.

"I don't understand it," Patterson's trainer, Dan Florio, was to say. "I didn't see what he got hit with. It didn't seem like anything."

Roy Cohen, Al Bolan and Tom Bolan were the main men in Championship Sports, Inc., promoters of the title bout. All three had excellent seats. But, outside Patterson's dressing room after the fight, they engaged in this bit of conversation:

"Al, did you see a punch?"

"No, but then I didn't have a good view. His back was to me."

Tom Bolan was asked a similar question.

"No," he said. "That's all, just no."

"How about you, Roy?"

"No. I just swallowed my tranquilizer, looked up, and he was down."

The three men who, most presumably, would know exactly what happened were Liston, Sikora, and—perhaps—Patterson (providing he'd seen the knockout punch coming).

Sonny said his left hand was the No. 1 howitzer.

"I knew the first time I jabbed him with it that he would be easy to hit. I connected with three left hooks, and that's the story.

"Soon after I connected with that first left jab, I threw a left hook that landed on the side of his face and he clinched. The referee said 'break,' and Patterson stepped back quickly.

8

"Then, we squared off again, and I threw a short right upper-cut. It was a good punch, very good, but he took it well. I followed it up with another left hook. It landed high on the head, around the temple, and he clinched again as he fell in toward me.

"This time, when the referee yelled 'break,' Patterson didn't want to. I had to push him off. He fell against the ropes and it was then that I realized he was hurt. He was stunned and his legs sagged.

"I hit him with the third left hook and he went down . . . The way he fell, I knew he wouldn't get up."

Liston's trainer, Willie Reddish had a word, he said:

"Those two rights to the body didn't look like much, but we knew that they hurt. Anytime Sonny hits you, it hurts, especially when he goes to the body."

"One minute, I had a fight," Sikora said, "the next, I didn't. I was all prepared to see them warm up. Suddenly, Liston landed a left hook to the jaw that turned Patterson partly around. Then came a tremendous *right* to the head and I had a new champion's hand to raise.

". . . I can say that of eight heavyweight title bouts I've handled, I haven't seen any more power than Liston showed me tonight."

Ashamed, embarrassed, humiliated though he was, Patterson didn't shy away from the task of talking to the press after the fight. He had already planned his flight into seclusion, but he talked:

"The right didn't hurt as much as the left hooks. I should have gotten up much faster. He surprised me with his fast start."

He was asked when he had picked up the "count."

"About five or six, I guess. I don't know which particular punch it was that did the damage . . . I didn't get a chance to get going . . ."

Patterson was asked if he was hurt.

"Just my feelings."

Did he think he'd been in condition to continue the fight?

"Sure, I thought I could go on," Patterson said. "But then, I guess every fighter thinks that."

Many people who saw the fight were quick to say that Patterson should retire. That opinion still held strong long after the bout was ended. But D'Amato had other ideas on the night of the fight.

"I definitely don't think he should retire," said Cus. "It wasn't as if he took a brutal beating. He told me later that he could see every punch coming, except the one that hit him. I definitely would tell him if I thought he should retire.

"After Ingemar Johansson took Patterson's title in 1959, D'Amato had been quick to predict that Floyd would become the first heavyweight to lose and regain the championship. But, after Patterson was kayoed by Liston, D'Amato did not make predictions so freely. "I could say that then," he explained, "because I saw then exactly what he had done wrong. He made a mistake, and mistakes can be corrected. But I didn't even see the punch tonight. I was under the impression that it was a right hand, but I hear now it was a hook. I guess I won't know exactly what happened until I see the movies."

A substantial number of outcries about the "quickie fight" were based on a fact no more complicated than this: the fans, particularly the one-hundred-dollar ring siders and the theatre patrons, had expected a longer battle, a "show," a contest. They felt cheated. Joe Louis, who had correctly picked Liston as the winner, touched slightly on the changing whims of the public.

"It's funny," Joe observed, "but when I knocked out Schmeling in one round, everybody thought it was a great fight and they were tickled to death. I told you what Liston would do to Floyd."

Joe didn't mention, of course, that he was a popular fighter, that he was, in a sense, carrying a national cause into battle, that—well, that he was well-liked.

Liston was hated.

The fact was, though, that Liston, while uncomplicated in his style and allegedly possessing one or two flaws in his "game," might well have given Louis trouble in Joe's heyday. But for his difficulties with the police, Liston probably would have beaten Patterson to the championship in the first place.

Another important answer to the easy conquest of Patterson is found in the fact that Liston was vastly underrated prior to this title fight. (Even Patterson, sometime later, said: "I could see practically every punch coming, but he threw so many *slow* punches!" To analyze that: the fight lasted but 2 minutes, 6 seconds. Only so many "slow" punches could be thrown in that length of time. The more likely prospect was that Liston was throwing fast punches but Patterson saw them in slow motion!)

As early as 1953, Tony Anderson, then head coach of the St. Louis Golden Gloves team, described Liston as "the strongest fighter I've ever seen, and I've seen them for more than thirty years. Although he's only had about six months of training, we've never had a heavyweight in Golden Gloves who was so good. The boy still is crude, and he's no Joe Louis—yet—but he's much faster on his feet and has more speed than Louis had at his age. In fact, he's one of the fastest big men I've ever seen. That's what most folks don't realize. They see how strong he is, but he's still awkward and he doesn't look fast."

"*But I could see practically every punch coming,*" said the conquered Floyd Patterson nine years later, "*but he threw so many slow punches.*"

There was still another angle to this fight:

Why did Floyd Patterson fight Sonny Liston, anyhow?

Managed carefully and cautiously by D'Amato, Patterson had rarely shown great inclination to fight the toughest men, the worthiest challengers. D'Amato didn't want the Liston fight and exhausted all his wiles in an effort to prevent it, even to the point of a reported break with Patterson himself. Patterson had gone along with D'Amato. Together they ignored Liston's challenge for a long while; then they set up severe standards which Liston would have to meet before they would even consider him. The Patterson team then drove such a hard financial bargain that Liston might very well have turned it down himself, except that he wanted the title bout so badly he probably would have fought for free, had that been the last resort.

Actually, though Liston has been characterized as being illiterate, he is by no means unintelligent. The personal campaign he waged to get Patterson into the ring was not nearly so flashy as was Archie Moore's campaign for a bout with Rocky Marciano, but it was more direct.

Patterson has been described as "a mental fighter." He was, and is, a sensitive, terribly proud man.

Sonny Liston hit him in the pride by simply stating that Patterson was afraid to fight him. Liston said, in effect, that Patterson was a coward. This upset Patterson so much, it is said, that he determined to fight Liston, somewhere, somehow, sometime.

(Did someone say, pride goeth before a fall?)

Then, during the pre-fight, training period, Liston employed another neat bit of psychology. He said that, as the champion, Patterson had to come out and fight. Liston said Patterson couldn't afford to run.

Patterson did come out . . .

But Liston himself credited United States President John F. Kennedy for "giving me a shot at the title." This is the story, as Liston told it, shortly after he had knocked Patterson out:

"It happened right after Floyd had knocked out Tom McNeeley in Toronto and I had kayoed Albert Westphal.

"The President saw both bouts on closed circuit television and said it would have been a better show if I had fought Patterson and McNeeley and Westphal had been matched.

"It was at that time that Patterson told President Kennedy secretly he had decided to fight me. I was the No. 1 challenger then.

"Frankly, I don't think Patterson would have fought me if he hadn't promised the President. I believe Floyd found himself in a position where he couldn't go back on his word. After all, you don't tell the President of the United States that you are going to do something and then fail to do it."

Now that Charles (Sonny) Liston is the new heavyweight champion, the cry already has gone up for him to rise above his unsavory past and bring "honor" to the crown. The Wheaties School of sports writers is pleading with him to mend his ways and be the kind of man "children can look up to," the very model of a proper hero.

This strikes us as arrant nonsense. First, it assumes that prize-fighters, regardless of their dispositions or past, are suitable objects for impressionable youngsters to idolize. Furthermore, if Liston suddenly is converted into a "good guy" for public relations reasons, it would be a dishonest trick to play on the youngsters. The biggest favor Liston could do for them is to act like the same heel all the pre-fight publicity said he was.

Why hoodwink the young hero worshipers into believing that only nice guys get to the top, or that a pleasant personality, a nice smile, and strict adherence to the Boy Scout oath are the way to get ahead in professional fighting?

Liston was in the ring for money. So was Patterson. Liston won because he is bigger, stronger, meaner and tougher.

As for his checkered past, including his association with the underworld, he's not the first prize fighter with this kind of background to make the big time and he won't be the last. That's the kind of business professional boxing is. It isn't fun and games, and the Epworth League is not the best training ground for a successful career in the ring. Liston is living proof of this (so, for that matter, was Jack Dempsey), and, as such, he is a typical representative of his trade.

—An editorial entitled *We'll Take the "Old" Sonny Liston*, in the Louisville Courier-Journal.

CHAPTER III

Sonny Liston survived rather well the tedious aftermath of his world's heavyweight championship victory.

He was suddenly a man in great demand, particularly for interviews. He was suddenly an acceptable celebrity whose presence was courted by representatives of many establishments. He was still a man forced under minute inspection. Some people carried on their inspection from afar, via telescope, as it were. Others used the microscope. What kind of man was he, really? Was he as bad as he had been painted, or was he merely a victim of misunderstanding? What kind of champion would he be? Could boxing survive with him as its king? Would the public forget his past mistakes and give him another chance? If the public gave him another chance, would he make the best of it? Would he give Floyd Patterson a rematch, as contracted? What kind of public figure would he be?

Interrogation ran rampant. Speculation was wild.

Prior to the fight, Sonny's wife, Mrs. Geraldine Liston, a pleasant, attractive woman who, obvious to all who saw them close-up, was the love of his life, had this to say about him and his career:

"If it were up to me, I'd never have let Sonny do it. I'd take poverty over prize-fighting. If we have kids, I won't let them fight, either. True, we wouldn't have the money. But if I didn't have it, I wouldn't know about it. And what you don't know about, you don't miss. "I'd much rather live simply without this anxiety and torment. Lots of people do things, and you don't hear about it. I know he's done wrong, but if he weren't in the public eye, it would be forgotten. The sports writers always keep bringing it up. It's like they don't ever want him to be good. How's a man going to be good, if folks don't let him? Many nights we talk it over. Sonny knows himself, and he knows if he becomes champ he only wants to live to make everybody realize he's a better person."

At this time—June, 1962—Mrs. Liston was asked if she'd be present when Sonny fought Patterson. "No! I get too nervous. I don't even listen on radio. I watch on television, until he's introduced and he walks to his corner, but when the bell rings, I turn it off. Once, in 1954, I watched. He knocked the guy out in the second round, but I couldn't stand it. The nervousness builds up. I sit there, moving my hands as though I were boxing, just as hard as he is. This will be the biggest night of his life (September 25, 1962), but there's nothing I can do except say my prayers so he doesn't get hurt. I'll just sit in the hotel trying to read a book and wait until his corner men call to tell me it's all over. If he wins, I'll give him the biggest, specialest kiss he's ever had."

Just as she'd said, Mrs. Liston did not attend the title bout in Comiskey Park. With her mother, Mrs. Eva Crawford of St. Louis, Mrs. Liston waited out the fight in their plush, tower suite at the Sheraton-Chicago Hotel. Her hair was up in curlers, cold cream covered her face, and she wore a bathrobe. She was ready to go to Sonny the moment he sent for her, but there was no listening to radio or watching television for Mrs. Liston. Female reporters occupied a portion of her waiting moments.

"Some people think he's mean and temperamental, but they're wrong," Mrs. Liston told Sheri Blair of the *Chicago American*. "He just doesn't like to talk much" . . . Georgie Anne Geyer of the *Chicago Daily News* heard her say: "If he wins, we'll feel it's God's will; if he loses, we'll feel it's God's will. I'm praying he'll win. Mostly, I'm just glad all this tension will be over." Contrary to boxing tradition, Mrs. Liston had joined her husband in his training camp, had maintained a close watch over his rigorous life there. Observers in camp—at the defunct Aurora race track—said "she is the only one who can handle him; he's like putty in her hands." As soon as he was finished with the fight, Liston gave an order: "Send for my wife!" When bodyguards came to the penthouse hotel suite to get her and take her to Sonny, Mrs. Liston was amazed to learn that the fight had ended so quickly.

"You're joking!" she exclaimed. "I didn't even have time to get nervous."

While more reporters and fans crowded around them, Sonny and Geraldine Liston went to dine in the Regency Room of the Sahara Inn, a club located north west of Chicago near O'Hare Field. Sonny was rather quiet, did not drink, but ate roast beef and a piece of "victory cake" and laboriously signed autographs (his hand dwarfing the pen to toothpick dimensions) while his wife helped him with the spelling of fans' names.

Among those present was the Reverend Edward Murphy, S.J., of Denver, a Catholic priest who was credited for a considerable amount of Liston's recent education and rehabilitation.

"Sonny will do very well," Reverend Murphy said. "I have no worries about him at all . . . I just have that confidence. He'll make a very good champion, he'll be a good leader."

"When you fight Patterson again," Liston was asked, "do you think you can take him out as quickly as you did this time?"

"Yes."

For Sonny, there was still more talking to do.

At noon on Wednesday, September 26, Liston held another press conference, this one at the Sheraton Chicago. Much of what he'd already said was warmed over. This conference was enlivened by the appearance of author Norman Mailer who said he "planned to prove in public debate that Patterson actually won the fight by a sixth-round knockout."

Liston said Mailer was drunk.

17

When the press conference ended, Mailer approached Liston and said: "You called me a bum . . ."

"I call you a bum," Liston said quietly, "and you are a bum. Everybody calls me a bum. I'm a bigger bum than you, because I'm bigger."

Liston held out his right hand.

"Okay, bum?"

Liston's display of a fine, subtle wit softened up critical reporters considerably. He had at no time resorted to overt braggadocio over his triumph. Matter-of-factly, he reminded all and sundry that the fight had ended just as he'd predicted. He was obviously grateful to Patterson for the chance to fight for the title; in fact, Liston defended Patterson against charges that Floyd had lost his "guts" the night of the fight. "That's got to be the stupidest thing I ever heard. I felt enough of him under my glove on that last hook to know it was a good enough punch to put any man down hard. I looked at him close when he was going down and I took another good look when he hit the floor. He was gone. He surprised me for a tiny second when he got up on one knee, but then I could see he was like a man reaching for the alarm clock while he was still asleep."

This side of Liston that came into view when he defended Patterson was no surprise to Willie Reddish, his trainer.

"I have been working with Sonny for three years," Reddish said, "and in that time I have never known him to do a mean thing. If he did, I wouldn't stay with him a minute."

Robert L. Burnes is the sports editor of the *St. Louis Globe-Democrat*. He was the man Father Alois J. Stevens, then the Catholic chaplain at the Missouri State Penitentiary in Jefferson City, called on over a decade ago while seeking advice concerning Liston's ability to become an established boxer. Burnes made contacts that eventually led to Liston's parole and his fighting career.

After Liston won the title, Burnes wrote a feature, the headline question being, "Will Liston Be Able to Shake His Past?" Burnes concluded that "time will tell." He wrote:

"Today, Sonny lives comfortably with his wife in a pleasant although not expensive home in a Philadelphia suburb. He likes fast cars and hot jazz but prefers mostly to sit around and loaf when he isn't preparing for a fight.

"A superb physical specimen, Liston could be the heavyweight champion for the indefinite future. There are no real challengers in sight. How wealthy he is, no one knows. Managers and others who call some of the shots for him remain unidentified. Most observers still believe that his boxing paychecks are cut up many ways before the residue comes to him.

"But he has money, he has a title, he has a future— none of which he had ten years ago when all this started. Those who dislike Sonny say he hasn't been rehabilitated at all. Those who like him [and while they are in the minority . . . are much closer to him] say that he has overcome the stiffest hurdles.

"Time will tell. Although his desire to have his past forgotten, will be respected, it will always be a shadow over his shoulder.

"If he stays close to those who have honestly helped him, this can be merely the start of a long and honorable reign."

During the Wednesday afternoon press conference in the Sheraton-Chicago, a writer asked about Jack Nilon, Liston's latest manager. The writer wanted to know, "Does he get paid?"

"Paid?" Sonny repeated. "If he's doing this for nothing, I want to thank him right here and now. From what I hear on TV this morning, *I'm* not going to get paid!"

Money had always been a sore point in Sonny Liston's career as a professional prize-fighter. In the early days of that career, beginning in 1953, he didn't earn enough to support himself, and his handlers were to say (while trying to explain some of his questionable managerial associations) that they couldn't afford the thirty-five dollars a week they were supposed to pay him when he wasn't fighting. In every one of Liston's fights, he was forced to accept the short-end purse.

The excuse was that Liston was "too good a fighter." In boxing, when a fighter earns that label, unless he's under magical management, he finds it tough to get fights with logical opponents, or often when he does, he must compromise on the money. Although Liston was solvent prior to the Patterson bout—he owned a home, a couple of cars, had money in the bank—he had quietly endured many financial humiliations. For example: when Sonny whipped Mike De John, he was paid only four thousand dollars, while Mike was paid three times as much. Patterson and/or his team of advisers had forced Liston to accept the lowest basic percentage imaginable (12½ percent) before they would grant him the chance to fight for the heavyweight championship.

Then Liston's share of the purse, as well as other fight monies accumulated by Championship Sports, Inc., was tied up in governmental action through an Internal Revenue Service lien. Liston's share of the revenue from the title fight amounted to more than three hundred thousand dollars. According to Nilon, he'd received only twenty-five thousand dollars for training expenses, several weeks before the fight. Patterson, according to reports, had received a much larger advance.

The Internal Revenue Service had decided to impound receipts from the fight following discovery that 1) Graff, Reiner and Smith Enterprises, Inc., a firm incorporated in Nevada in 1961, which organized the closed-circuit television showing of the fight, had effected a deferred-payment plan with Championship Sports, Inc., without seeking an Internal Revenue Service ruling; and 2) neither Graff, Reiner and Smith nor Championship Sports, Inc., had filed tax returns covering the year 1961.

Six weeks before the fight, Internal Revenue Service officials began planning the unprecedented seizure of the multi-million-dollar gate from the Liston-Patterson fight for tax purposes. Ironically, the Internal Revenue Service's meticulously arranged timetable for the seizure was thrown somewhat out of kilter when Liston demolished Patterson so quickly.

Revenue officers had been told to wait until 10:30 P.M. on the night of the fight to notify operators of two hundred and sixty theatres across the country that they were to turn over to these governmental agents all box office receipts due organizers and promoters of the fight. Liston had, of course, ended the fight before 10 P.M.! Internal

Revenue Service officers had no difficulty collecting gate receipts at the park, but others were forced to employ ingenious delays to keep theatre managers in their offices forty-seven minutes after the fight ended, in order to serve the order.

The Internal Revenue Service officers—operating under a legal proviso which empowered the Internal Revenue Service commissioner to demand immediate payment of taxes due if he knew or believed that a delay might jeopardize collection—seized upwards of four million dollars.

Liston took this "financial turn of events" with good grace, even to the point of cooperating with a wire service photographer who set up a gag-shot, showing Liston standing on a Chicago street, suitcase in hand and trying to "thumb" a ride out of town. But, as late as October 22, 1962, the Liston camp revealed that no satisfactory financial settlement had been made.

Under the by-line of Jack Cuddy, United Press International reported out of New York on October 22 (1962) that "heavyweight champion Sonny Liston, angered at being forced to go on tour to get 'eating money,' announced today he will break away from Championship Sports, Inc., and make his first title defense in February against Floyd Patterson. Through adviser Jack Nilon, Sonny made his announcement which designated the new sixteen-thousand-seat Baltimore Civic Center as a preferred site for the return fight with Patterson. Nilon said Sonny would break loose from Championship Sports, Inc., for alleged breach-of-payment contract and make his first title defense under a new promoter.

". . . Nilon charged today that Championship Sports, Inc., failed to give Sonny $50,000 within 48 hours after the Chicago fight, as contracted. Nilon added, "And the rest of our estimated $282,000 purse was to have been held in escrow until after Liston gave Patterson his return title shot, within a year (under this contract, which gave Patterson every conceivable break, even after he lost the title, Patterson was to suffer no less than a 30–30 split of receipts and was privileged to dictate the site of the bout!)

"The only money Liston received from Championship Sports, Inc.," United Press International story continued, "was $25,000 for

21

training expenses, given him at the time he signed the formal Illinois Commission contract in Chicago, weeks before the fight." (Nilon said.) Cuddy stressed, "I haven't heard of Championship Sports, Inc., putting any of Sonny's money in escrow . . . because the government is holding up practically all funds connected with the bout—in a $2,175,500 lien."

"But the slender, brown-haired adviser emphasized that he believed the government's lien had nothing to do with the plans of Championship Sports, Inc., to pay Patterson his proceeds from the fight at intervals over 17 years. "In my opinion, the United States Government doesn't do business this way," Nilon continued. "There is much more to the government's lien than meets the eye—matters that have nothing to do with the recent fight."

The story revealed that Liston had refereed a fight at Portland, Oregon; was scheduled to referee another at Houston, Texas, and was considering "eating-money" exhibition tours in the Orient and Europe. Concerning Nilon's statements, according to Cuddy, Tom Bolan, president of Championship Sports, Inc., made this comment:

"Championship Sports, Inc., has not breached its contract. If Nilon thinks we did, we'll have to let the courts decide whether or not we did." Bolan said that a New York representative of the Internal Revenue Service had told him recently that "a release of funds is imminent."

When Liston, his wife, and Nilon returned to their Philadelphia home two days after the fight, some fifty well-wishers met their plane at the airport on a rainy day. Airport officials sought to steer Liston through a private passage to an interview room, but Nilon nixed the plan because "the people want to see you, Sonny." Sonny smiled, embraced his wife gently, and said a few words. He assured listeners that the winning of the championship wouldn't cause his head to swell. In this context, he said: "I'm going to be the same guy and do the same things." When he was asked how he was fixed for money, in view of the government's lien, Nilon spoke up: "We'll make out. We won't starve."

But Sonny was not yet out of the woods. Two days after he arrived home in Philadelphia, one of his home town newspapers, the

Philadelphia Inquirer, carried a story under New York writer Dick Young's by-line, and Young said, in part: "The sham that Liston has divorced himself of unsavory handlers is tissue-thin. Jack Nilon, the respectable businessman who supposedly calls all shots for Liston, is no more a boss than the president of Russia, whoever he is.

"Nilon doesn't seem too perturbed about the prospect of not getting paid right now. The day after the fight, following the discussion of finances, he shrugged and said: 'I'm not worried about the money. We came to Chicago for one thing, the title, and we got it.'

"Liston got it. He will be an exciting champ. He plans, after disposing of his return bout commitment to Patterson, to defend the title four times a year. He'll fight when the mob tells him to fight— and that will be often. He'll be 'good for boxing,' as the guys write it— and as they wrote that Patterson was not. But boxing will not be good for Liston—not as it was for Patterson. Sonny will be cut up six ways to Christmas. He doesn't have an altruist like Cus D'Amato to look after him and to make sure the money is there in the name of Sonny Liston after the title is gone.

"Liston figures to be champ for a long while. Nobody is around to take it away from him; certainly not Patterson. When Floyd first lost the title to Ingemar Johansson, I felt he had been smitten by a lucky punch, and that he would beat Ingo next time out. I'm just as convinced he wouldn't beat Liston if he fought him 20 times—with a gun."

Meanwhile, New York, which had refused to sanction a Liston-Patterson title bout there because of Liston's alleged associations with unsavory characters, was now forced to consider recognition of him as the world's heavyweight champion.

Action by the New York State Athletic Commission was forestalled by the New York State Joint Legislative Committee on Boxing. Claiming it had "important evidence linking Liston with the underworld," the committee held a hearing. A little-known heavyweight named Cortez Stewart testified before the committee that on April 7 (1962), Blinky Palermo, a former fight manager also known for his underworld connections, had promised to "move me along fast" if he (Stewart) would work as a sparring partner for Liston while Sonny trained for Patterson. Stewart said he wasn't aware of whom Palermo was when the offer was made. But he identified Palermo from a photograph. Stewart claimed that "the man" refused to meet his demands for $50 a day, the alleged excuse being that Liston was in debt and couldn't afford Stewart's price.

The committee subsequently invited Liston and his "managers of record" to come to New York and "comment on, affirm or deny" the testimony rendered by Stewart. In Philadelphia, Nilon said, "I don't even know the boxer (Stewart). I don't know Mr. Palermo." He said he thought Stewart was a publicity-seeker. Later Liston, through an attorney, declined the invitation to go to New York and testify before the committee. The grounds were essentially the same as those mentioned by Nilon.

The New York Athletic Commission then announced that Sonny Liston was being recognized as heavyweight boxing champion of the world but that it wasn't yet ready to grant him a license to box in that state. "He must earn that right," the commission said.

Mexico reneged on its welcome when a proposition was advanced to bring Liston to the capital of that country for a series of exhibition matches. Jet magazine, reporting this action, said: "Mexico has categorically shut its doors and removed the *bienvenido* (welcome) sign for Sonny Liston. No reason has been given for this by officials of the State Department's Migratory Division. But (the) unofficial view is that the boxer would set a bad example for Mexican youth.

"It was learned that promoter Miguel de la Colina presented a strong appeal to the Federal District Boxing Commission, asking that the fighter be permitted to appear in exhibition matches in the Mexican capital. Luis Spota, head of the Commission, rejected the plea on the basis of: "The commission is collaborating with Senator Estes Kefauver and his United States investigating committee. Sonny Liston [who once appeared before Kefauver's Senate investigating committee, therefore, is on the "prohibited" list.' "

Police were still watching Liston's movements. Less than two weeks after he'd kayoed Patterson, Philadelphia's Fairmount Park police picked Liston up. No charge was made. He'd simply been driving "suspiciously slow" through the park. Shortly after that, Mr. and Mrs. Sonny Liston were back at the Sheraton Chicago Hotel. They were hunting property, they said. Mrs. Liston told the author that they wanted to buy "a ten-acre place." As usual, Sonny didn't have a whole lot to say. But he did say that when they found a suitable home in Chicago they were returning to Philadelphia to pack up and move out of that city immediately.

While researching the Liston life story for this book, I went to the Missouri State Penitentiary at Jefferson City to talk to Warden E. V. Nash.

A former schoolteacher and Missouri highway patrolman, Nash was not warden at the time Liston was there in the penitentiary. But Nash, a forceful, erudite man, was familiar with the Liston record. As I saw Liston, apparently having been harassed out of his second city, seeking a new home in Chicago, I recalled a few of Warden Nash's words:

"He was just another man in here serving his time. He didn't bother anybody and nobody bothered him. . . .

"By virtue of the fact that he's been in a penitentiary . . . it all comes back again. . . .

"Why not recognize the fact that he's served his time? . . .

"They constantly 'ex-convict' these fellows. . . .

"They can't be branded for the rest of their lives—unless they brand themselves. . . .

"We're our brothers' keepers. But we're poor followers of our own teachings. How many ex-cons have you invited to church in the past five years?"

If they're big enough to go to the dinner table, they're big enough to go to the fields.
—The late Tobe Liston, father of Sonny Liston, talking about his children.

CHAPTER IV

The aftermath of the Liston-Patterson title fight confirmed a point all the pre-bout hubbub had established so indelibly: Liston was, without a doubt, America's most controversial athlete.

Whether he was good for boxing or bad for boxing—the subject of serious debate before and after Patterson—was now the basis for heated arguments and editorials from one end of the country to the other.

As one facet of Liston's life after another was revealed to the public, the controversy was fanned into fiercer flames by—the many inconsistencies and the numerous variances of detail. There never seemed to be—and you shall see it again in this chapter—any one set story about a single vital facet of this man's presence on earth, excepting that:

Sonny never had it easy.

Sonny's life was always cloudy.

Sonny's life had always been rugged, rough, squalid, dark, dank, depressing.

There was pitifully little sunshine in his life, pitifully little about his life that was encouraging. But, was Sonny Liston's rugged, squalid life excuse enough to justify the things he'd done?

Mrs. Helen Liston, now sixty-four years of age, mothered eleven children, six of whom are living, including E. B. Ward, born before her marriage to the late Tobe Liston. Tobe Liston himself reputedly fathered twenty-five children in two marriages. When she was asked if any of the others had ever committed a crime, she said:

"No. It hurts me when I think about the trouble Sonny's been in. I think he fell in with the wrong people."

But, then, what does this prove? It could be that Sonny was the one child of all the Liston children who required more from life than the others.

Regardless, it must be admitted that what life offered him was nothing bountiful.

Forrest City, Arkansas, is located about fifty miles west of Memphis, Tennessee. You take the Memphis Arkansas bridge and follow Highway 70 through West Memphis on out into the farm country. It's the wide, open spaces, and there doesn't seem to be a whole lot stirring. Soon you notice these skimpy little houses— skimpy, little frame houses, many with wrinkled, tin roofs; some set close to the highway, others dotting the vast acreage. The lawns are plain dirt and this is where little barefoot kids in their Lil' Abner clothing play. If a front door is open, you try to peek in as you pass by, but it's like trying to see inside a cave without a light. In the front yards, or to the sides, of several of these houses, you see the metal carcasses of dead cars. The ones that're running, with motors and recent license plates, are vintage models. Clothing hung out to dry flap in the breeze like multi-colored flags. You see little evidence of paint and the modern conveniences are conspicuous by their absence. This is Saturday afternoon, and not a lot of work is going on and this is the reason, you suspect, that the kids are so free to play on those dusty front yards. It could be that there's something to this kind of living— hominy grits and ham hocks and chitlins—but there isn't much to recommend it. Then, you subtract thirty years of "progress" from what you see, and you're back in the time and atmosphere when Sonny Liston was born, for his home was right around here.

Mrs. Helen Liston lives with her son, E. B. Ward, and his wife, in a small, white, spanking-clean house in Forrest City, Arkansas. Mrs. Liston lives there on the specific invitation of her daughter-in-law, and, with use of "mother wit" with which Sonny too is richly endowed, she explained that "I wouldn't go to live with any of my sons unless their wives invited me to come. When you go without the wife's invitation, if there's trouble later, the wife is liable to blame it on the mother-in-law's being there. I would never go live with a son on his invitation alone." Mrs. Liston, spry for her age and cordial, keeps house for the Wards while they tend the cotton-fields. It was obvious from the bright appearance of the Ward home, which is nicely furnished and well equipped, that, given a house to care for, Mrs. Liston is a wonderful housekeeper.

There is a great deal of Sonny in her, appearance wise. Although she is much shorter than he is, as her late husband also was much smaller than Sonny, they both have the same large heads, sturdy necks, strong, massive shoulders, chests, arms. In the long, muscular arms of Mrs. Liston one could read years and years of man type toil. She wears eyeglasses but her brown eyes twinkle as she talks about her children—her life and theirs. She speaks in a deep voice; she speaks often of "the Lord," of her faith, of being blessed by his gifts of free air and rain. Although she declares herself not to be "much of a speaker" in public, she handles herself extremely well in an interview; she is not reluctant to talk, nor is she cagey or evasive. She sprinkles her conversation with little homilies, such as these: "It's not good to listen to too much gossip—there's too much talk going on"; "talk's easy done, but it takes money to buy land."

Mrs. Helen Liston, like her late husband, was born in Montgomery County, Mississippi. Theirs were farming people. Her parents were James and Martha Baskin. His parents were Alexander and Fanny Liston. Helen and Tobe Liston moved to Arkansas in 1916. They subsequently rented—or sharecropped—land from a Negro farm operator, Pat Heron, in St. Francis County, Arkansas, near Forrest City. "The bossman got three fourths of what you raised," Mrs. Liston explained. "We raised cotton, corn, sorghum molasses, peanuts, sweet potatoes, hogs, cows, chickens, and we had a garden. We had to raise what we ate and then buy shoes and clothes."

When was Sonny Liston born?

"I think," said Mrs. Helen Liston, "it's the 18th of January, 1932. I know he was born in January, in 1932. It was cold in January.

"We had a shabby, little, old four-room house and it was cold. I was attended (at his birth) by a mid-lady. There was never any such thing as a doctor when I was raising my children.

"He had the same appearance that all babies have when they enter the world. But I noticed his big hands when the mid-lady brought him to me, after she'd dressed him.

"I said, 'Ain't he got big hands for such a teeny-weeny baby?' She said, 'He's going to be a boxer.' I wish she was alive today. She'd be proud that her word came true.

"He (Sonny) was a good child.

"He was about as good a conditioned child as I had." Mrs. Liston's six living children are Sonny, the second youngest; Wesley Liston, the youngest, who lives in Cherry Valley, Arkansas; Curtis Liston and Mrs. Annie Wallace, who live in Gary, Indiana, where Mrs. Liston also lived during most, if not all, of the time Sonny was in serious trouble in St. Louis; Mrs. Alcora Jones of St. Louis, and E. B. Ward. "He loved to play. He liked to play with me. He was obedient to me. He never fought back. He's still obedient to me."

Recalling her husband, Mrs. Liston said:

"He was awful thin. I'm five-foot-one and he was five-five. I had an uncle who was tall," she said, explaining the likelihood that Sonny took his height from an other side of the family. "My mother was a tall woman. There were tall people in my husband's family.

"All my children grew fast. They were healthy children. I made them go to bed early. They didn't have any television to watch until 12 o'clock at night. My children ate their food, washed their feet, and went to bed after it got dark."

Mrs. Liston was asked if Sonny went to school when he was a child in Arkansas.

30

"He went a little bit, whenever his daddy would let him. But his daddy always had a job for him and the others to do, rain or shine. Their daddy put him out there to work as soon as he (Sonny) was eight or nine. He said if they (the children) could go to the dinner table, they could go to the fields.

"He (Mr. Liston) didn't whip them as much as people say he did. But he hollered at them a lot. The biggest thing he did was whoop and holler. He whooped and hollered so much nobody paid any attention to him."

Mrs. Liston herself decided to leave the Arkansas farm and seek another job—she'd always worked in the fields right beside her husband—in the city. She left during World War II.

"Our crop was short one year," she explained, "and I could hear the news on the radio that help was needed in St. Louis and they'd pay you while you learned. So I figured this was a good chance for me to learn something else. I knew my husband wasn't going to leave the farm. So I went on up there and got me a job in a shoe factory.

"There wasn't too much of a problem about the children getting taken care of. I didn't have but one little fellow that needed to be taken care of he was six years old—the rest of them could make a day."

After Mrs. Liston left Arkansas, "Sonny stayed there on the farm for a while. But he followed me to St. Louis [according to Sonny's account, he arrived in St. Louis when he was thirteen, which would place the year at 1945]. He arrived at night. The police put him in a place where I could find him. The police in St. Louis will take care of a child . . . !"

It was interesting to hear Mrs. Liston make this complimentary remark about St. Louis police, who figure so strongly in another side of Sonny's life. Monroe Harrison, who was associated in the early management of Sonny, also mentioned a night "when the police picked him up. He was very young. He was sleeping in an alley. They took him down to the police station, gave him a place to sleep, fed him bologna and crackers. They kept him with them three days. They liked him—he did little chores around the station—and he liked them. He didn't want to leave . . ."

31

Back to Mrs. Liston's story of Sonny's arrival:

"He moved in with me. I had two rooms to myself, upstairs in a house. I finally had four of the children with me altogether. We lived on O'Fallon Street. We stayed one time on 16th Street . . ."

Mrs. Liston thought Sonny should go to school in St. Louis.

"I started him out going to night school," she said. "I got him in and I'd go with him some nights to see that he did go. If I didn't go with him, he'd go to the show, sometimes. He didn't go like he should have.

"I also got him a job at a poultry house. Then he worked on an ice wagon a while . . .

"I'm not sure how he happened to get into so much trouble. I guess it must have been the company he kept. You know, it's sometimes the company you keep which run your luck into a bad string. He was just a country boy. He didn't know to do nothing. But they was picked up and he was picked up, too . . .

"He confessed religion in the Methodist Church. Here in Arkansas. I heard him confess. I used to tell him he had to cultivate his religion. He said he would."

Mrs. Helen Liston admits that she had no special ambitions for Sonny because "you can't choose how other people can live their lives. But I wanted him to live in the glory of the Lord. And I believe he's going to get it. I want God to get the glory out of his life—and, then, I'll be happy!"

A few months prior to the Liston-Patterson title bout in Chicago, Allan Morrison of Ebony magazine had this to say:

"If Floyd Patterson is ever to be dethroned, the man most likely to accomplish that feat is a mean-looking, cunning, powerful hulk named Charles (Sonny) Liston. A misfit most of his life, Liston, twenty-nine, is a man who believes he was cruelly short-changed when the breaks were handed out. Even today, standing on the threshold of wealth and prestige undreamed of a dozen years ago, he remains an over-grown boy, given to practical jokes and sudden bewildering shifts of mood. He is a man in a hurry and his goal is the heavyweight

32

championship of the world. 'I want to be champion because the money is important to me. I'm not after a whole lot of money. *I only want to be comfortable for the rest of my life and provide for my family.* But the honor of being champ is also a big thing.'

"Those words reflect the outlook of a new Liston, a man chastened by life's tragedies and dogged by the furies ever since he can remember. He was always too big or too poor or too black, the boy from a broken home who never got enough love and was continually left out of things. His suspicions linger and the old bitterness sometimes wells up in him, but he is now less withdrawn. Violence is still the one language he speaks most eloquently. But he prefers to act out his strong hostilities in savage barrages of punches in the ring."

Boxing became an avenue of expression, a means of re-directing the vast anger that lies within him. Long before he began fighting professionally, he was a fighter and society was the enemy. He says that in the old days it seemed he was always fighting with his back to the ropes and the odds were so heavily against him that he had no chance of winning.

"When he enters the ring to fight Patterson, he will be a strong favorite to take the title. There is a faint smile on his lips when he realizes that for the first time in his life the odds have been reversed in his favor."

Liston told Morrison: "My father was a farmer. I worked the fields—corn, cotton, hay." Continuing the Ebony story, Morrison said: "It was for him a time of back-breaking labor and unpleasant parental discipline. His relationship with his father was tense and cold and undoubtedly helped to embitter him. There were regular beatings too, severe and painful. Once, after a particularly unsparing whipping by his father, he ran away. He returned, but only to face another whipping. When his father abandoned the Liston brood and his mother moved to St. Louis in search of employment, Charles followed her there. There was no father in that home, little discipline, and only the barest suggestion of love. He became a tough kid who ran wild in the streets. He does not like to evoke memories of his boyhood. 'I had it tough as a kid,' is all that he will say about that period in his life."

While approaching the same general topic—Liston's past—Senior Editor Sam Castan said in *Look* magazine:

"Liston's past and the metronomic regularity of his difficulties with the law have earned him many enemies. Overriding opinion, particularly among influential sports columnists, holds that he has placed himself beyond the redemption historically offered by boxing to men who have strayed. An opposing view is held by the few close friends, and fewer journalists, who have managed to poke through his reticence and know him well. They find an honest, touching side to the boxer and see him as a basically decent man, who, until recently, was cast as one of life's losers by circumstances he could neither control nor fully comprehend.

"Charles Liston was born on *May 8, 1933*, in a rickety backwoods shack near Pine Bluff, Arkansas. He was one of the twenty-five children of a field hand. At thirteen, he fled to St. Louis, where he enrolled himself in the first grade and was immediately laughed out by classmates for his size and country mannerisms. At 18, illiterate and bitter after a hand-to-mouth existence in the back streets of St. Louis, he was sentenced to five years in the Missouri State Penitentiary for armed robbery. He was paroled in the care of Father Alois Stevens, a prison chaplain who perceived innate good in him. But a few years later, Liston was back in prison, following a fight with a policeman. While in St. Louis, Liston was picked up for 'questioning' over a hundred times and arrested fifteen times on charges ranging from breach of the peace to suspicion of theft—all without conviction. On the two occasions he was convicted, he served a total of thirty-eight months."

In the *Philadelphia Bulletin* five days after the Liston Patterson bout at Chicago, Charles Chamberlain, an *Associated Press* sports writer, told this story:

"Sonny Liston is a man with two records—one inside the ring and the other outside it.

"The best thing that could have happened to him was to win the world heavyweight boxing championship, a mantle he insists he will wear with dignity.

"Many will berate him as the hoodlum heavyweight, branding him with his past records of arrests and two jail terms. Many will say he has paid his debt to society and let him look ahead to the future, walk among men with his head high.

" 'I have reached my goal as heavyweight champion,' says Liston, who came from a broken family of 25 children amid the squalor of an impoverished cotton patch in Arkansas.

" 'When you reach your goal, you represent something and you have a responsibility to live up to it. " 'There was a time when I was convinced I would never get out of the jungle I once lived in. In those days, I didn't care what I did and had little regard for the feelings of others because I thought everybody was against me. I realize now that a man can't be successful or happy with that attitude.

" 'As champion, I can do something good for somebody else.'

"If Liston's past can be forgotten—and not filed away for reference—then he can be taken on his word."

Chamberlain's article in the *Philadelphia Bulletin* continued:

"He has proved himself inside the ring and he seems to realize that maybe his biggest fight now is establishing himself in the eyes of many outside it.

" 'I have been in the limelight two ways—good and bad,' says Sonny. "Right now I'm in the good limelight, but there are people who don't want me to be there. Regardless of them, I intend to stay there and I promise everyone that I will be a decent, respectable champion.

" 'I intend to model myself after Joe Louis, who I think was the greatest champion of all and my idol. He did everything I want to do. I intend to follow the example he set and would like to go down in history as a great champion, too.

" 'I have accepted all the punishment dealt to me for the mistakes I made when I was growing up. I had nothing when I was a kid but a lot of brothers and sisters, a helpless mother, and a father who didn't care about any of us. We grew up with few clothes, no shoes, little to eat. Ever since I was born, I've been fighting to stay alive, to make a place for myself and live a reasonably normal life. I've never been able to do it. I am probably closer to it now than I have ever been.' "

Liston's childhood was also the lead concern of an *Associated Press* article, which said:

"Sonny Liston knows he has a lot to live down before he can live it up as the world's new heavyweight boxing king.

"This massive man of many moods has become America's most controversial athlete because of his past. As champion, he promises to wear the crown with dignity. He has many good qualities that could be used to outweigh the bad.

"Liston, who never made a real effort to learn to read and write until about two years ago, was a victim of environment, of squalor, that made violence his strong point both in and out of the ring.

" 'You know what I often wonder about?' he says. '*Where* were all these people who work with kids when I was growing up?

" 'For the first thirteen years of my life, I lived like a heathen on a cotton patch in Arkansas. I hated home, and I hated school. My father was married twice. The first time, there were twelve children, and I remember none of them. I was one of thirteen born in the second marriage.

" 'My father worked me hard and whipped me hard. If he missed a day, I'd feel like saying: "How come you didn't whip me today?"

" 'Not long after my mother left and went to St. Louis, I followed her. I was thirteen then. I was real big even then. School? That wasn't for me. The kids made fun of me because I was so big, and I would start fighting.

" 'I got a job with a construction gang. Those guys treated me like a man. They thought I was one because I could work as hard and as long as they could, and I could do more than hold my own in a fight.

" 'It was a tough bunch. Many of them had been in jail and others were headed there. But they were the only friends I had, and they influenced what I did and thought. I never knew there were other kinds of people.' "

Milton Gross, the *New York Post* sports writer and columnist who helped Floyd Patterson write his book, *Victory Over Myself*, once said of the new heavyweight champion:

"Sonny Liston was one of 25 children in a broken family. He cannot write anything but his name (June, 1961). Once when he was asked by the Kefauver Committee if he could write the address where he lived, he answered, 'No, sir.' He was asked next: 'Suppose your share of a fight purse was $25,000 and they handed you a check for it. Could you tell whether they were giving you a check for $25,000?

" 'Not exactly, Liston answered.

" 'How much education did you get?' Senator Kefauver asked.

" 'I didn't get any, Liston said.

" 'You didn't go to school at all?"

" 'No, sir.' "

Ray Brennan is a famous *Chicago Sun-Times* writer. He is best-known, perhaps, for his crime stories. For reasons that will, we think, be obvious, *Chicago Sun Times* editors assigned a Liston feature to Brennan prior to the title bout. In part, Brennan wrote:

"Until nearly two years ago, at the age of about 28, he (Liston) never made a serious effort to learn to read and write. Violence has been his forte, both in and out of the ring.

"Boxing authorities call him a great, natural fighting machine. Hitting people and getting into trouble would seem to be his two main talents.

"Still, there have been clergymen, boxing writers, decent people in the active fight game, and others who have found fine qualities in Liston. With effective guidance, he had done good work among juvenile delinquents.

"Liston was born on a semi-barren cotton patch near Little Rock, Arkansas, in May, 1932. He believes he had 12 brothers and sisters and that his father, a share cropper, had 12 other children by a previous marriage.

"At the age of 13, young Liston, wearied of being beaten by his father, ran away to St. Louis and joined his mother, who had fled the cotton patch earlier."

A month after he won the world's heavyweight title, Liston revisited Chicago. One day, while looking for this author, he made a pop call at Johnson Publishing Company. He was closely observed by two female members of the staff. When the three of us talked about it later, this was the gist of what was said:

"He's very shy, isn't he?" one lady asked. "I think he's bashful."

"I don't know about him being so bashful," I said. "He just doesn't talk much. His mother says he never did talk much. She says he has a sister in St. Louis, Alcora, who is the same way. She says that on the night he won the title fight he called her—his mother, that is—and asked how she was. Mrs. Liston told him, then asked how he was. 'He said he felt fine; he was just a bit tired. He asked how I was doing. I told him.' Then, he said, 'Well, I'll be seeing you,' and that was all."

"I think he's very *sweet*," the second lady said.

"*Sweet?*" I asked in astonishment.

"Yes—sweet," she insisted. "He reminded me of Joe Louis. He talks a lot like him. I think Joe Louis is handsome . . ."

"Do you think Sonny Liston is handsome?"

"Well . . . er . . . ah . . . I wouldn't say Sonny Liston is handsome, but I do think he's sweet!"

In the various narratives of Sonny Liston's purported early life, at least three different birth dates were as signed him. His mother told me: January 18, 1932. Sonny himself said it was May 8, 1932. (Yet much of the pre-fight publicity quoted his age as being 28.) There was another report that he was born on May 8, 1933.

Sonny was born on this farm in St. Francis County, Arkansas, near Forrest City. But his birth place was listed variously as being Pine Bluff, Little Rock, and "near" Little Rock. One explanation was that, early in his professional boxing career, someone decided that it would be better to list a large town or city near his actual birth place, *as his birth place*, rather than stick to the whole truth. Pine Bluff apparently received most of the votes.

These were the *consistencies*:

As a mere tyke, he went to work in the fields. Life was rugged. He received little, or no, education. His father had a large family by two wives, the second being Sonny's mother. (In reply to a question, his mother told me: "No—I never remarried. *I'm just Helen Liston.*" She did not variate her assertion that she had mothered 11 children, 10 by Tobe Liston, and that one of her children, E. B. Ward, the eldest, was born "while I lived at home with my mother." Mrs. Liston displayed no bitterness whatsoever toward the late Tobe Liston, defended him—as said—against the charge that he whipped the children unmercifully, praised him as a "hard-working" man, and made only one complaint of any importance: "That man loved the farm; he'd never leave the farm . . .")

But there was—particularly in Sonny's opinion—a dearth of love for the kids.

Although there are certain aspects of Liston's life he apparently wishes to have forgotten, this can be said in his favor:

He hasn't been reticent in discussing his past, at least, once he's started talking about it, he hasn't. Liston is the chief authority for stories about his poverty as a child, and he has not attempted to deny his involvements on the wrong side of the law. "If you want to know something about me," Liston said once when he was irked with a writer whom he thought had by-passed him in search of information, "just ask me."

When Liston sat down with writer Wendell Smith of the *Chicago American* to write a serial about his life, he made this plain:

"In the beginning, I want to emphasize that I have no intention of copping a plea in this presentation concerning the problems and troubles I have encountered during my life. I am a mere human being who has made some terrible mistakes, all of which I regret. To say that I did not know better is no excuse. Some of the things I did were inexcusable, others were committed because I was influenced by people in whom I was foolish enough to trust and believe."

This is a straight-forward, honest, and logical statement. What more would Liston's critics have him do? Even those who discount the influence of environment in the formation of a person's character must admit that Liston had fewer opportunities than most to learn "right side up" and he had more opportunities than most, particularly after he became a big-money-potential fighter, to go wrong. Liston has asked, "Where were all those people who work with kids when I was growing up?" This is a fair question. *Where*, indeed, was the helping hand for the kid Charles Liston, who was big and strong enough as a young teenager, as was Jack Johnson, to hold his own with full-grown men in the toughest physical jobs and in the rough-and-tumble of brawling? Warden E. V. Nash, during a conversation with the author, pointed out that when a man spends considerable time in prison, many of his friends, if not all of them, are likely to be convicts and ex-convicts. A man seldom steps out of prison into so-called high society. How many "responsible citizens" are there to meet and greet an ex-con on his release on a man-to-man basis and take him to church, help him land a job, build a new, constructive life? How many will stick with him after they've learned, on the job, during a meeting of a church committee, in a social club, that *this* man has done time? Prejudices are not only racial. But, in Sonny's case, it seems fair to conclude that racial prejudice compounded his difficulties. Yet the ex-fighter Rocky Graziano, lately a television star, admits that "compared to me, this guy (Liston) was an angel." And Liston himself, making pointed reference to a sensational boxing incident involving light heavyweight Harold Johnson a few years ago, has said: "I never ate no bad oranges."

While telling his own story, Liston has said:

"I have accepted without whimpering all the punishment dealt to me for the mistakes I made voluntarily when I was growing up. The others, which were the result of bad advice from insincere associates, disturb me greatly because now I find it hard to believe that I was such an easy sucker for their schemes."

Suckers in boxing are legendary—and almost all of them blast up through the bedrock of unfortunate circumstances to the fame and fortune most of them are unable to handle, especially the finances, primarily because they've had no prior experience with fame and fortune. Archie Moore had his brushes with the law when he was young. He was rehabilitated, or he rehabilitated himself, while locked up for his mistakes. Yet, though Moore has admitted his past and written about it himself, none of this is thrown up in his face today. He is a living legend. As Liston himself has noted in some wonderment, not all of Jack Dempsey's early life was exemplary, but today Dempsey is, possibly excepting Joe Louis, the most popular boxing personality alive. Primo Carnera was exploited unmercifully by gangsters; for one of his bouts, which involved many thousands of dollars, Carnera received only a pittance, thirty-five dollars.

Although in recent years the sensational exposé of youthful indiscretions has become an increasingly popular facet of personality profiles and/or published biographies, the incidence of a criminal background in a Negro's life seems to command more attention and comment than it does in the publicized lives of whites. A criminal background often is treated as special spice in the popular downbeat approach of Negro living. When Hollywood would hardly treat any Negro subject objectively years ago, prison scenes were integrated. There generally seems to be more integration in misery than in painless existence. Poverty, tough luck, are no excuses for wrongdoing; but the fact is that criminality and poverty, particularly slum-dwelling in major cities, run as an entry.

Continuing his story, Liston has said:

"Looking back over the years, I can understand the reasons for my failings. When I was a kid, I had nothing but a lot of brothers and sisters, a helpless mother, and a father who didn't care about a single one of us. "We grew up like heathens. We hardly had enough food to keep from starving, no shoes, only a few clothes, and nobody to help us escape from the horrible life we lived.

"When I hear people say this is a 'hard, cruel world,' I know exactly what they mean. Ever since I came into this world on May 8, 1932 in Pine Bluff, Ark., I've been fighting to stay alive, to make a place for myself and live a reasonably normal life. I've never been able to do it. I am probably closer to it now than I have ever been."

You will note that, in this story, Liston mentions Pine Bluff as his birth place. An explanation of this discrepancy has already been written herein. In Forrest City, Mrs. Helen Liston said: "He's never been there, I'm sure. I've never been there, either." She explained that when Sonny turned pro, his manager told him to "put down a pretty big town" as his birth place and, "for some reason," he "thought of Pine Bluff." This is a fairly common fabrication.

Back to Sonny Liston:

"The people who don't need friends are those who have plenty of everything—money, food, clothes, and an education." Not exactly the fact of life but understandable thinking, nevertheless, like another Liston gem, "There are only two kinds of people—good and bad, right?"

"I didn't have any of those things [money, food, clothes, an education] when I was a kid. In fact, I never went to school regularly. I am just now reaching the point where I can read well enough to figure out the most ordinary stories in the newspapers. My wife, Geraldine, has been a big help along this line, and in other things that I missed long ago.

"I never had the opportunity to attend school more than two months in succession. I had to help out around that little plot of ground we grew cotton on. They didn't force kids to go to school in Arkansas, especially colored kids.

"Not only that, but I was ashamed to go to school with the other kids. It wasn't much of a school, of course, but still I didn't want to go because I didn't have the clothes that a kid should have to attend classes every day.

"I was extremely large for my age. I was almost twice as big as the other kids my age. They used to laugh at me, poke fun at me. I resented it. I felt out of place. Even on days when I could get away from the cotton patch, I'd skip school and go wandering off someplace else.

"I hated home. I hated school. My father was married twice. The first marriage produced twelve children, none of whom I remember. I was one of the thirteen children born of the second marriage. How do you live in a situation like that without money?"

On another occasion, while momentarily depressed, Liston said:

42

"So-called 'good people' talk about some of my friends and their background. I know one thing. When I needed a few bucks to feed my . . . brothers and sisters, my friends gave me the money. Where were the 'good people' hiding then? Do you think any of them would have given me a five-dollar bill?"

Momentary sound-off recitals such as this haven't done Liston any public-relations good. This is obviously a defensive remark, laced with sarcasm. The fact is that Liston knew none of the notorious "bad people" in his life when he was a boy back in Arkansas.

Liston does not publicly admit to ever knowing fear, either as boy or man. This fearlessness in him was a quality noted in the context of his Chicago fight with Patterson, that helped establish his favorite position. The closest he ever came to fear, Sonny has said, was one night in Arkansas when he was a boy.

"It was one night when me and my brother was walking toward the river. The moon was so bright it looked like day and when we came to the top of a hill, we saw a man walking back and forth—only he didn't have any head.

"Me and my brother stopped sudden-like and my brother says, 'Where's his head at?' But he don't wait for an answer. You'd hear about ghosts and haunts and such things, but *I wasn't really scared*. I was just running to keep my brother from being scared."

Liston was just entering his teens when he decided to run out of St. Francis County, Arkansas, which was, for him, a "ghost area," if not haunted. Mrs. Helen Liston had made good her escape from the farm, although she was to return to "make two crops with the kids," not including Sonny, before returning North again, this time to Gary, Indiana. Mrs. Liston arrived in St. Louis, Missouri, in 1944 or 1945—World War II was in its homestretch. Sonny says he was thirteen years old when he followed her there.

Having no money, he stole.

He stole enough pecans to purchase a bus ticket to St. Louis, where bigger crime and bigger trouble were already scheduled for him by Destiny.

The inconsistencies in various accounts of Sonny Liston's life were mentioned previously.

Liston has blamed these inconsistencies on the press. Which is not exactly a unique explanation. Many celebrities take this approach when questioned closely about seeming discrepancies in their histories.

With a swish of his finely honed razor of sarcasm, Liston has said:

"The press don't write the truth. They said my wife was pregnant; they said she's thirteen years older than I was; they say that she goes around here and I don't count; they almost had her in the corner fighting."

While commenting on this charge against the press by Liston, writer Leonard Shecter said in the *New York Post*:

"If these are the only inaccuracies which have appeared in the great volume of material which has appeared about Liston . . . he's lucky. Such is the nature of fame and the American press. Actually, though, this is flyspeck hunting. Liston doesn't care all that much about typographical errors which turn a three to thirteen. He does care about the new image he's trying to build of himself and that does not contain his record of nineteen arrests and two prison terms."

After he had moved from St. Louis to Philadelphia, Liston was asked once if he intended to revisit his old home city.

"I've already got nineteen," Liston said. "I don't want twenty."

"He was just a country boy."
—Mrs. Helen Liston

"He's the champion now. He should be grateful. He should be even more grateful he's alive. That was one bitch of a town then. Believe me."
—A St. Louis detective

CHAPTER V

In St. Louis, Sonny Liston was out of his element.

He had traded the wide-open spaces and the slow pace of Arkansas for the cluttered, slummy, asphalt jungle of a big city. He was a stranger there.

He was a boy, though big as a man, walking into a lion's den, hardly knowing lions hung out there; he was like an "innocent" in a den of thieves. "It was a year after the war when the . . . kid with the man's body first showed up around the alleys of St. Louis," Pete Hamill wrote in the *New York Post*. "He was looking for his mother," one St. Louis detective who knows him said, "and he found her. But he also found a town of con-men and hustlers, drifters and pimps, the flotsam and jetsam of a war . . . a town where a big kid could get jammed up. *It was the town that spawned Sonny Liston.*"

When Sonny arrived in St. Louis, he was awed and he was naive. He was looking for his mother, and he thought it would be A—B—C simple to find her.

"I figured the city would be like the country," he has said, "and all I had to do was to ask somebody where my mother lived and they'd tell me she lived down the road a piece. But, when I got to the city, there were too many doggone people there, and I just wandered around lost. But one morning I told my story to a wino, and he says I favor this lady that lives down the street."

This lady, so Sonny's story goes, was his mother. Mrs. Helen Liston told the story of his arrival somewhat differently, tossing a bouquet to the police.

If the search for his mother had taken Sonny into a fine neighborhood, where she either lived or even "worked in service," Sonny could, at least, have seen how the other half lived and, speculation is, he might have been inspired to reach up, over his head, grab a limb of the better life, and pull himself out of his rut.

But, the search for his mother led him to the slums of St. Louis, where even today the rough brick streets in some of these St. Louis parts will shake bolts out of your car and rattle your bones while you're riding and, though slum clearance progresses, ridding the scene of some awful eyesores. There the dank, rusty houses, apartment buildings and warehouses, covered with the soot of many coal-burning winters and much manufacturing, must have been a sorry sight for this thirteen-year-old country kid who was seeing it all for the first time.

This was 1946.

When Liston appeared before a Senate committee headed by Estes Kefauver of Tennessee, who was investigating underworld control of boxing, he was asked:

"What did you do when you got to St. Louis?"

"Well," Liston replied, "my mother put me in school, and then, after I got started going to school, other kids seen me coming out of—I was such a large boy—other kids would see me coming out of such small kids' room. So they would make fun of me and start laughing and I started fighting. Then I started playing hooky, and from hooky, I led to another thing, so I wound up in the wrong school."

"What school did you wind up in?"

"Well, the house of detention."

"How old were you then?"

"I was about 14."

"How long did you stay there?"

"My mother, she got me out, and then, well I figure— she got me out and I went right back for the same things."

"You did what?"

"I went back to the same thing and wound up in a bigger house this time."

While collaborating with Wendell Smith of the *Chicago American* in his by-line story just prior to his fight with Patterson, Liston threaded this story further: "After drifting around St. Louis, from one place to another, I got a job with a construction gang. The other workers treated me like a man, not the boy I was. They thought I was a man because I could work as hard and as long as they could.

"Well, I don't need to tell you that they were some pretty tough men. Many of them had been in jail and others were to eventually wind up there. But they were the only friends I had. They were my associates. They influenced my life, the way I thought and the things I did. I never knew there were any other kind of people.

"I'd heard of Negro doctors and lawyers, and outstanding businessmen, of course, but how was I going to get with them? They were educated, refined people. I wasn't educated and knew that I wasn't refined . . .

As far as "refined Negroes" were concerned, Sonny Liston never had a chance! On the night Liston fought Patterson in Chicago, the *New York Post* assigned writer Ted Poston to "ringside" in Harlem at Loew's Victoria Theatre. Leading off his story next day, Poston noted this immediate reaction to Liston's victory:

"The stocky, conservatively dressed man half rose from his seat in Harlem's packed Loew's Victoria Theatre and his soft words carried far beyond his elevated box seat. He said, simply:

"'God help us.'"

"And in the stunned silence of at least 20 seconds, he seemed to speak for over 2,500 Negroes in their $6.75 seats, for the hundreds of standees ranged behind, for scores of others crouching in the crowded aisles and for dozens of teenagers who had slipped through a back door, dashed from behind the TV screen and lost themselves in an earlier joyful crowd, only half-heartedly chased by the cops.

"For Loew's Victoria belonged to Floyd Patterson for two minutes and five seconds last night. And no bad man in the worst melodrama had been hissed and hooted as wildly for the same length of time as was a villain named Sonny Liston."

After making notes on crowd-reaction at Loew's Victoria Theatre, Poston went over to the Hotel Theresa in Harlem where, almost traditionally, Negro fight fans congregated for post-bout communion and spirits and sidewalk ogling in the Joe Louis era, the Sugar Ray Robinson era, and later.

"The Hotel Theresa's corner at Seventh and 125th, which Joe Louis owned a dozen times, had not a single celebrant," Poston reported. "Not a single Black Muslim on a step ladder on any of the other corners.

"One lonely straggler paid a reluctant tribute to the new champion.

" 'No other Negro in all history,' he said, 'has so united his people in a common hope—the vain hope that he'd get his block knocked off.'

"Harlem had an early curfew last night."

Before the fight, Sonny Liston was talking to Wendell Smith, and he was saying:

". . . I wasn't educated and knew that I wasn't refined . . .

"You can look at yourself and tell just about where you fit in. I fit in with the construction gang. They spoke the only language I knew. It was tough language, but I could speak it with the best of them— and I could fight the best of them and hold my own."

Liston learned early in St. Louis that his best friends were his fists.

48

"It's Sonny's hands that always got him into trouble," a St. Louis writer has said. "Nobody realizes what a temper this guy has. Why he has the temper, I don't know; but he has it. And when you get a guy with hands like his, and a temper to trigger them, you got trouble. Sonny says that first charge was a truancy charge. I heard it was for busting up a couple of smaller kids."

This is what the detective was referring to:

Shortly after he arrived in St. Louis, Sonny was arrested. The very first year there, this was. There is some mystery about what Sonny actually did. Some say he committed an assault. Anyway, he was given a lecture and was released to his mother.

This brush with the law didn't scare Liston out of "mischievousness." Monroe Harrison, who was to become big in his life, has mentioned an incident, which may, or may not, have been the one above. Harrison said that, on this occasion, Liston took five dollars from another boy who had been sent to a store to buy groceries. "He was fifteen years old when he got his first major rap," Harrison said, adding: "He was hungry."

Liston fell in with a gang of kids who meant nobody any good. When he was about sixteen, he and his gang pulled a caper and were nabbed by the police. As Liston has said:

"We broke into this restaurant about two in the morning and got away. But, after we'd gone ten blocks, we decided to stop and get some barbecue, and then the police came along and barbecued us."

Again, Liston was released on probation, but, by this time, he was a two hundred-pounder, he was immensely strong (Harrison has recalled that one time Sonny lifted up the front end of a Ford, just because someone said he couldn't do it!), quick-triggered with his fists, characterized as being "evil," and called, in his gang, the "No. 1 Negro."

By January of 1950, Liston was pretty well immersed in crime. He was arrested for six muggings, one that brought just a nickel. Liston, and his companions, also were charged with the robbery of a luncheonette.

"Suddenly in the area in which Liston and his gang stalked, there occurred a series of muggings," writer Gene Courtney said in the *Philadelphia Inquirer.* "One victim was struck in the mouth, knocked down and robbed of six dollars. A second reported three men beat him and dragged him into an alley where they relieved him of nine dollars. A third was pulled into an empty lot and forty-five dollars was taken forcibly from his billfold.

"Liston and his juvenile delinquent friends had found another outlet for their energies. It was daring; it was physical but it wasn't very profitable.

"As in any form of education, the good student gets promoted. Sonny and his cronies were good . . . and so, naturally, they advanced to armed robbery."

Liston once explained his activities this way:

"We were just always looking for trouble. Someone says, 'Let's stick up the restaurant' and we did. We never got a chance to count the loot. To this day, I don't know how much there was in the haul. There were four of us, me and three other kids, and we never split it up or anything. We just did the job like the stupid, crazy, bad kids we were."

In 1950, Liston hit a real snag.

A St. Louis service station was robbed. Two people were beaten for no apparent reason. Liston was caught. He was sentenced to serve concurrent, five-year terms in the Missouri State Penitentiary at Jefferson City. The convictions were obtained on two counts of robbery and two counts of larceny.

"In my opinion," a St. Louis policeman has said, "going to the can was the best thing that ever happened to him. If he hadn't gone to the can, he would never have met Father Stevens and if he never met Father Stevens, he never would have learned to box, and if he hadn't learned to box, he'd be dead of a bullet in the back."

Liston himself has admitted, "If I hadn't gotten in trouble, I'd never have become a fighter."

Mrs. Helen Liston has said:

50

"I had already left St. Louis when he got into trouble. They say he confessed . . . I don't know."

Mrs. Liston went from St. Louis back to the Arkansas farm, "made two crops with the kids," and then headed North again to live in Gary, Indiana, for eleven years. She was not a part of the historic events that started Sonny off on the road to the world's heavyweight championship!

A man can learn something beneficial and useful in an institution . . . Sonny learned boxing. That's his trade. And he's progressed at it. There's no use to keep reminding him that he's an ex-convict. Nobody knows it better than he does. There's no need to keep all the pride and manliness that was knocked out of him when he came here— knocked out of him. Let him go and be world champion, as long as he conducts himself properly.

—Warden E. V. Nash, Missouri State Penitentiary

CHAPTER VI

The story of Charles Liston's incarceration in the Missouri State Penitentiary at Jefferson City is composed of one part fact and one part legend, which may also be fact.

Liston entered the prison on June 1, 1950.

In June, 1952, he was "released" to the prison farm, a semi-trustee, minimum-security auxiliary unit located about ten miles outside Jefferson City, the state capital.

On October 30, 1952, he was paroled into boxing.

Since that time, Liston has returned to this particular pen only once, on a visit, about a year before he dethroned Patterson.

While discussing Liston with the author after the Liston-Patterson title bout in Chicago, Warden Nash said, "I can bring two hundred men into this office and they'll all tell you that they were Sonny Liston's cell mates." But the truth is that prior to the beginnings of his prison boxing career, Liston wasn't especially famous inside the big-house, which was populated with more than three thousand men, a third of them Negro, two thirds of them Caucasian.

According to prison authorities, he was no disciplinary problem. Once or twice, the records now show, he was reprimanded for shooting craps; on another occasion, he was chastised for "hollering in the line."

He was enrolled in the prison school program for a brief period of time, but dropped out. "At that time," Warden Nash has explained, "the program wasn't what it is now. Now they have civilian teachers with degrees. Then there was one civilian instructor and the others were good inmates.'"

Many facets of the Missouri State Penitentiary are better today than they were in Liston's time, partially as a result of a national riot, in 1954, when more than eight million dollars' worth of property was destroyed and life was lost; largely because of the enlightened program conducted by Warden Nash, a stern, forceful, frank, yet humane person who believes "we're our brothers' keepers" and declares that "we try to give them [the prisoners] something tangible." Currently, Jeff City prisoners are permitted various means of learning and recreation. They are racially segregated while eating and sleeping, but all other facilities are integrated.

W. P. Steinhauser, a huge, friendly man who is now Assistant Warden, worked at the penitentiary during Liston's time and remembers him:

"As well as I can remember, Liston was assigned to the kitchen and worked on the docks—where they bring the vegetables in and unload them from the farm. He got started boxing under Father Stevens. He was just a big, stout man. His arms were as big around as my legs. He was a pretty slow starter (in the ring). It seemed that it'd take him a couple rounds to get started. But I don't think you could hurt the man. Whenever Liston hits you, it's just too bad . . .

"He wasn't too much of a mixer here. He was a re served sort of fellow. He was the sort of fellow you almost had to draw a conversation out of. We had no trouble with him at all. He was all right. When he was here, very few even thought of him as being a potential world's champion."

Andrew Lyles says he did. Lyles says he was serving a burglary sentence at Jeff City in 1950 when Liston was brought in. "I guess I was the onliest one back then who said Sonny was going to be a champion," Lyles told the *Associated Press* after Liston kayoed Patter son. Lyles said he spent more than a year in the same cell with Liston. "He's just shy," was Lyles' personality appraisal. "Of course, if he don't like you, it was pretty tough to get close to him."

Fact and legend merge and the story moves on:

A former boxer, an inmate named Joe Gonzalez, is credited with nicknaming Liston "Sonny." Originally, Gonzalez, who tried to interest Liston in boxing, called him "Sonny Boy," but eventually the moniker was shortened to "Sonny."

Legend declares that Sonny Liston became an in-prison champion of the Negro race before he became heavyweight champion in the ring. As this colorful saga goes:

The Jeff City prisoners were divided into gangs. A man named Hank Calouris ran the Westsiders; Nick Baroudi ran the Italians; and a convict simply known as "Frankie" headed the Eastsiders. These three groups ganged up on the Negroes.

Liston resented it and, so the story goes, one day he walked across the prison yard, hit Calouris with the back of his hand and said, "I'll do that every time I hear you touched a colored boy. If you don't like it, I'll see you in the hole at six." He hunted Baroudi and Frankie and told them the same thing.

Liston had selected "the Hole," a storage room beneath the cells, because it was the only place they could fight without being disturbed.

Five minutes after the four began fighting—three on one—Liston came out, leaving Calouris, Baroudi, and Frankie in beaten hulks on the concrete floor in the Hole.

There is another prison fight story: "Taunted by older inmates, Sonny flew into a rage, became embroiled in a vicious fight with one of the tougher long-termers. 'I told Sonny,' Father Stevens is quoted, 'that this sort of thing could only extend his sentence. With his physique, I invited him to try out for the prison boxing team.' "

When I contacted Father Alois J. Stevens at the church he now heads in Southwestern Missouri, I told him of the fight story above and also mentioned that the records read to me at the Missouri State Penitentiary failed to substantiate these stories. Father Stevens asked me if I had been shown a "yellow record sheet," and I told him, no. I repeated the fight story attributed to him, and he said: "That's been so long ago. I don't want to put the writer on the spot who wrote the story. *But I don't remember the incident.*"

Father Stevens was the prison chaplain. He was also the prison's recreation director. The most popular sport was baseball, but boxing and wrestling were big during the winter months.

"At first," Father Stevens said, "Liston was just one of many (participating in the boxing program). But he developed so fast that it wasn't long before we realized his potential."

Boxing matches were held in an auditorium which was destroyed in the riot as well as in the prison yard. Three or four boxing shows were arranged each year for the inmates; one or two were open to the public from Jefferson City. "Aside from training sessions," Father Stevens said, "I would guess that Sonny had eight or ten bouts. I think he went through two seasons there."

Having been impressed by Liston's potential, Father Stevens conceived the idea that he might be a professional prospect. "I didn't say very much to Sonny until I talked to Burnes (Robert Burnes, Sports Editor of the *St. Louis Globe-Democrat*, which, at that time, sponsored the annual Golden Gloves tournament in St. Louis). There was no need to 'rev' the kid up until I could see what I could do. But he was willing to go along. Sonny doesn't talk much now. He was less talkative then . . ."

"What about Sonny's intelligence, Father?"

"I think he's a pretty intelligent boy. He's no fool. He's not dumb by any means. He just never had a formal education. But he's pretty shrewd. He has a great sense of humor. He learned to write his name and a few other little things in Jeff City. But he could count money. He learned that a long time ago."

Burnes listened to Father Stevens' story, to the proposal. "He was willing to give it a try, anyway."

A former fighter who had once been a Joe Louis sparring partner also, Monroe Harrison, was closely tied in with the *Globe-Democrat's* Golden Gloves program.

"Burnes had Harrison in mind as Sonny's manager," Father Stevens said. "But Harrison worked as a custodian at a school in St. Louis and didn't have any capital. He brought in Mitchell (Frank Mitchell, now publisher of the *St. Louis Argus*, a Negro newspaper, and also a man who managed fighters). The way I understand it, Mitchell would contribute the capital, while Harrison would handle the fighter."

Before anyone was to make a serious move on Liston's behalf, it was decided that he should be tested by a professional heavyweight.

As Frank Mitchell told the author:

"Bob Burnes scratched his head and tried to figure who would be the best man to take to Jeff City to test Liston in a fight. Bob Burnes called Monroe Harrison. Monroe Harrison called me. I had a stable of fighters. I was to be the bankroll man, if this thing worked out. Tony Anderson, a veteran trainer, was consulted. He knew fighters. He could spot them—snap!—like that! Tony took the best heavyweight in St. Louis to Jeff City for this scouting trip on Liston."

The fighter selected to "test" Liston was Thurlow Wilson. Included in the group that went to Jeff City were Anderson, Harrison, Mitchell.

When the fighters were ready, Liston was asked: "How many rounds?"

"Don't make no difference to me."

"Make it five or six rounds," Wilson said confidentially. "He won't last that long."

In the first round, Liston started jabbing his left. "He had a terrific left hand even then," Anderson has recalled. "He was born with it."

"He had a great left hand but no right hand at all," Mitchell told me.

"He had a right hand," Anderson said, "but he was afraid to use it because of the tremendous power he had."

After two rounds, Wilson called it quits.

"I don't want no more of him."

After the brief session was over, Wilson thoroughly roughed up, Harrison told Father Stevens: "You found me a live one."

"Get him," Anderson advised Mitchell. "I can make a champion out of him."

"It was my recommendation that clinched it with Mitchell," Anderson told me. "Liston was a good, strong boy and he had all the potentialities."

Mitchell promised Father Stevens that day, "You'll hear from me."

"I got him paroled," Mitchell told me, "got him a room at the Pine Street YMCA and a job with a steel company. He worked during the day and trained at night.

"We entered him in the Golden Gloves that February (1953). He left-handed everybody out of the Golden Gloves. In Chicago, he romped right through until he met [the late] Ed Sanders. He was scared to death of Sanders but he beat hell out of him. He romped all the way through the Golden Gloves. No contest."

During my talk with Father Stevens, this point was clarified: Liston, he said, was paroled to Mitchell and Harrison, not to him, but to Mitchell and Harrison.

"I usually had to stay out of those things," the Father concluded.

"He's the grandest fighter I've ever handled. I thought a wonderful lot of the boy and I still do."
—Tony Anderson

CHAPTER VII

In St. Louis today, Frank Mitchell, Monroe Harrison and Tony Anderson are three men who, like many others like them in the sport called boxing, know how it feels to let a "big one" get away. There remains some controversy over how Liston got away from Mitchell. Harrison admits that he couldn't carry his share of the financial load and sold out to a druggist named Eddie Yawitz. Mitchell, too, declares that Liston, the fighter, was too heavy an expense for him to shoulder and that he, subsequently, sought help. Anderson, who put in seven years' work with Liston [he drew 10 percent of Liston's purses as his trainer's fee, after Sonny turned pro, while Harrison and Mitchell operated the managerial end], is somewhat bitter about the way things turned out.

"He wasn't a bad boy," Anderson said. "He was badly misused. I could bawl him out in my way of bawling him out and he'd be all right. But you couldn't push him around like a dog.

"He was a fight-handler's dream. I only had to push him to get rid of an opponent. He could have stayed here in St. Louis and done the same identical thing. They ran him away from St. Louis. He didn't want to leave St. Louis."

Liston made a sensational career's beginning in St. Louis. Less than a year after he'd been paroled out of Jeff City, he was nationally known among the amateurs.

Other fighters have fought more amateur bouts than Liston; Cassius Clay for one, but none has ever been more spectacular.

Under the watchful eyes of Anderson, Mitchell and Harrison, Liston trained religiously in the gymnasium at the Masonic Temple on Olive Street and also at the Ringside Gym. His basic, stand-up, style; left foot flat, up on the ball of the right foot; capitalizing heavily on strength, advantages of reach; and—of course—what was, almost from the beginning, the best left jab in boxing since Joe Louis' heyday, was soon fashioned.

One of the earliest news stories involving Liston appeared in the *St. Louis Globe-Democrat* on February 1, 1953, prior to this newspaper's eighteenth annual Golden Gloves tournament at Kiel Auditorium. The writer was Raymond V. Smith, who said:

". . . Heavyweights, usually the smallest group of the eight weight divisions in the open and novice departments (of the Golden Gloves) will be plentiful. Rated topnotch contenders are Percy Davis, novice runner-up to Millard Smothers, who moves to the open field, and Charles (Sonny) Liston of the Ringside Gym . . ."

Four days later, Smith reported the outcome of the Golden Gloves fight between Liston and Luther Corder of Jackson, Tennessee:

"Charles (Sonny) Liston, a sharp-hitting heavyweight from the Ringside A.C., lowered the night's curtain and the boom on Luther Corder . . . to gain the final with Leroy Willis of Ft. Leonard Wood."

A later story said:

"Charles (Sonny) Liston, the big Bertha from the Ringside A.C., who draws Lloyd Willis in the open heavyweight bout next week, hardly worked up a good sweat in knocking out Luther Corder, his semi-final opponent . . . in the second round."

The Golden Glove finals were held on Friday night, February 13, 1953, with 15,449 fans in attendance at the arena. Smith reported:

"The show . . . came to a spectacular close when Liston, a member of the Ringside Gym, came back in the last two rounds to win a unanimous decision over All-Army Champion Lloyd Willis of Fort Leonard Wood.

"Willis looked like he might be an early winner when he nailed Liston with a flurry of ether-packed leather, but Liston, a slow starter, shook them off. Charley took command in the second and in the third battered Willis into a groggy mess."

Tony Anderson was head coach of the Golden Gloves team.

On the same page with all the news was published a one-column cut, showing a lean-faced Liston, a pleasant, new moon of a smile creasing his visage. The St. Louis Golden Glove winners were entered into the Midwestern Golden Glove Championships at Chicago. The team, Liston included, of course, left St. Louis by train at 8:58 A.M. on Saturday, February 21, 1953, headed for Chicago.

In the February 24 issue of the *Globe-Democrat*, Jim Lubbock reported:

"Spearheaded by heavyweight Charles Liston's third round TKO of his first opponent, St. Louis Golden Glovers roared through the second night of the Midwest Gloves championships with a perfect record of eight victories out of eight fights . . .

"In becoming the first St. Louis battler to score a knockout or TKO in this year's tourney, Liston displayed the same stunning straight left and terrific strength he has shown in winning the St. Louis championship.

"After a few seconds of the first round, it became apparent that the only question of the outcome was whether Liston's opponent, Donnie Fleeman of Fort Worth, could go the three-round route.

"Fleeman is a good boxer, and fairly fast for a heavyweight, but he caught too many of the St. Louisan's lefts to the head. He seemed quite willing to call it a night when the referee stopped the fight after forty-six seconds of the third round."

Liston fought a second bout that same evening, winning a decision, and Lubbock reported:

"Liston's second fight matched him with Carl Mc Clure of Oklahoma City, and the local heavyweight got in some good licks to the body, which took most of the starch out of the Oklahoman. McClure managed to last out the fight, but was pretty wobbly at the final bell."

The pattern which Liston had established in the beginning with Thurlow Wilson had been revealed to the public during the St. Louis Golden Gloves, and it was now being seen by Chicagoans. Sometimes, Liston started slow, but always managed to get his man. When he failed to knock them out, he left them pulverized. (Harrison has recalled how Liston handled Wilson at Jeff City: "Sonny beat Thurlow so bad. He knocked some of his teeth out. Wilson still has the gold replacements in his mouth") Although Liston had been fighting less than a year, he was already capable of meeting and defeating "experienced amateurs." When they hit him their hardest blows, he merely shook them off and kept on boring in, the sledge-hammers flying.

Tullos Lee Mead of Memphis was reputed to be a knockout artist when he arrived at the Chicago Golden Gloves meet in 1953. But, scoring one of the most sensational triumphs of the championships, Liston toyed with Mead for a round and a half and then smashed him with long lefts to the head and rights to the body until the referee decided that he (Mead) had had enough. After Liston destroyed Patterson at Chicago, Mead recalled the Golden Gloves match and said ruefully, "When Liston knocked me down [the first time], I made the mistake of getting up!"

Liston was the sole St. Louis survivor in the Chicago, or Midwestern, Golden Gloves Championships. In his semi-final match with Ben Bankhead of Kansas City, Liston again started slowly but came on strong in the second and third rounds to earn the decision. Bankhead clung helplessly to Liston's mid-section at the end.

In the finals, Liston dethroned Ed Sanders of Los Angeles to win the Midwestern Golden Gloves heavy weight title. [Sanders, who was to die tragically following a professional bout, had won the Olympic Games heavyweight championship at Helsinki, Finland, in 1952.] The *Globe-Democrat* called Liston "St. Louis' newest amateur sensation." In a story that carried no by-line, the Globe-Democrat said:

"Liston, boxing only seven months, whipped the 6-foot-4 Sanders with some stout in-fighting. His victory gave St. Louis a second-place tie with Oklahoma City with 18 points . . ."

On March 22, 1953, the *Globe-Democrat* carried this story:

"Four men will represent St. Louis in the National AAU Boxing Championships in Boston this year. Heading the list is Charles (Sonny) Liston, Midwest Golden Gloves champion, who added the Ozark AAU title to his collection . . . without firing a shot. All his opponents defaulted!"

And, on March 26, 1953, Lubbock wrote:

"The Golden Gloves heavyweight champion of America is Charles (Sonny) Liston of St. Louis.

"In winning his fourth amateur title in the last two months, the powerful, young St. Louisan . . . hammered out a decisive point victory over highly touted Julius Griffin of New York in the national champion ship gloves matches at the Chicago Stadium.

"Griffin, a knockout artist nicknamed 'The Hammer' by Eastern sports writers, *knocked Liston down early in the first round*, but that was his one big moment in the fight.

"Liston who was apparently more caught off balance than hurt, came back strong for the remainder of the round, and gave better than he got just before the bell ended it.

"In the second round, the St. Louis steelworker began to fight along lines familiar to all who saw him in action in St. Louis. He bashed and shoved Griffin again and again with his long left to the face, following with rights to the body and head. In spite of the New Yorker's vaunted punch, Liston got the better of several brief but vicious exchanges toward the end of the round.

"The final stanza was pretty much all Liston . . .

"Liston's victory was particularly sweet to St. Louis rooters, because the published opinions of both Chicago and New York sports writers have been that Griffin wouldn't have much trouble winning."

Apparently, St. Louis was proud of Liston, who weighed two hundred and four pounds, at this juncture. And well it might have been. In the brief period that he'd been fighting, he had won the *Globe-Democrat's* St. Louis Golden Gloves heavyweight title, the Midwestern title, the Ozark AAU title (by default), and the national championship.

During the National AAU tournament at Boston in April, 1953, Liston knocked out his first opponent, Lou Graff of Detroit, in fifty seconds of the second round. *But he lost the first bout of his career to Jim McCarter of Philadelphia on points. "Against Jim McCarter, a clever fighter,"* said a news report, *"he couldn't find the range . . ."*

In June of 1953, the *Globe-Democrat* sponsored the International Golden Gloves matches, pitting the St. Louis Golden Gloves against Europe's best amateurs. The June 22, 1953, issue of the *Globe-Democrat* carried this story:

"Charles (Sonny) Liston, besides being the most powerful man ever to come out of the Golden Gloves here, has the unique ability to be able to stand up under a punch that would ordinarily stagger a water buffalo.

"Liston virtually breezed through the 1953 Gloves campaign. At the time, he possessed little more than a left hand. A good hook to the body and a jab that must have felt like running your face into the blunt end of a four-by-four carried Liston to the championship. *"Since that time, however, Charley has developed a right hand that fairly whistles. In his last good workout . . . Liston gave professional heavyweight Stan Howlett a good working over and ended up slashing Howlett's left eyebrow.*

"Early this year, Liston worked out with the 230-pound Nino Valdes, as the big fellow was preparing for a bout here with Archie Moore.

"Valdes, at the time, the quicker of the two, stepped in and caught Liston flush on the chops with a good right. Liston never blinked his eyes and sailed into Valdes with a tremendous body attack that had the huge Cuban giving ground."

Liston brought St. Louis a five-all tie with the European boxers during the International matches at Kiel Auditorium, St. Louis, by scoring a first-round technical knockout over Herman Schreibauer of West Germany. And Robert L. Burnes, who had played such an important role in Liston's boxing career, wrote:

"The crowd of 7,849 . . . jumped to its feet, grabbed for its hats and headed for home when Liston, after being puzzled momentarily by the southpaw tactics of Schreibauer, started a potent body attack. When Schreibauer's guard went down, Liston's attack went up and a terrific right put Herman on the canvas.

"He staggered to his feet at the count of nine, but was groggy and referee Vic D. Filippo, after one look at him, wisely stopped the fight two minutes and 16 seconds after it started."

Someone said Liston had "whistled while he worked" on the German.

It was said now that Liston had begun fighting in September, 1952.

He had been paroled from Jeff City in October, same year.

He had won five amateur titles, losing but one bout, suffering only one questionable knock-down.

His handlers decided—and they had pretty good reason—that it was time Sonny Liston turned pro.

Sonny Liston is the strongest fighter I've ever seen. Once I saw him pick up the front end of a Ford—pick it right up off the ground . . . showing off! Somebody said he couldn't do it.
—Monroe Harrison

CHAPTER VIII

In the neat, wood-paneled publisher's office at the *St. Louis Argus*, Frank Mitchell, a small, lean man, threw one leg up on the edge of his desk, made himself loungingly comfortable in a swivel chair and—in a husky, baritone voice—talked about Sonny Liston's beginnings as a professional fighter.

"His first professional fight was a four-rounder with Don Smith at the St. Louis Arena. Sonny kayoed him with the first punch of the first round."

The date was September 2, 1953.

This was the beginning of a brilliant record, in which Liston was to win fourteen of his first fifteen bouts leading up to an enforced layoff because of an alleged assault on a St. Louis policeman. He won seven by knock out, seven by decision.

Mitchell and Harrison had signed him to a two-year contract with a two-year renewal option. It was agreed that they would subsidize the fighter to the tune of thirty-five dollars a week when he had no fight income or no job. Even this piddling amount was to prove too much of a financial burden for Mitchell and Harrison, they now say, and it was this money problem which, according to Mitchell, led to later contractual arrangements with "questionable characters." It will be interesting to note, as the story is told, that Liston apparently had little, or no, say-so about the deals through which Mitchell and Harrison, certainly Harrison, divested themselves of their interests.

All beginning fighters start off at the bottom of the financial ladder. Half a hundred dollars is about average for the professional neophyte while he is fighting those first few preliminary bouts. Mitchell and Harrison hardly made a profit, considering normal training expenses, and, thus, they have a story to tell, too.

Liston's first five professional bouts were fought in St. Louis.

Fifteen days after he disposed of Don Smith, he won a four-round decision over one Ponce DeLeon. On November 21, 1953, he decisioned Benny Thomas in six rounds.

On January 25, 1954, Liston knocked out Martin Lee in six rounds, and, on March 31, 1954, he decisioned Stan Howlett in six rounds.

Now, the managers decided, Liston was ready to take on more serious competition, out of town.

Mitchell resumed telling the story:

"One of his most important wins was over the highly touted Johnny Summerlin of Detroit.

"I made the match. Meantime, the trainer (Tony Anderson) was working on Liston's right hand. His left hand was almost perfect then.

"In Detroit, there was talk that Summerlin would knock Liston out in two or three rounds. But when people saw Liston in the gym, the odds began dropping. Liston won a unanimous, eight-round decision.

"This fight proved to us he could take a punch.

"In the early part of the sixth round, he got a little careless and got hit. Real good. But he took all Summerlin could give him and went on to win. In their return bout, Liston won again, by a wide margin. He became popular in Detroit. He was matched next with Marty Marshall."

Sonny won the two eight-round decisions over Summerlin at Detroit on June 29 and August 10, 1954. He fought Marty Marshall at Detroit on September 7, 1954, and suffered the first loss of his professional career. But though Liston also suffered a broken jaw, Marshall couldn't knock him off his feet.

"I was busy with the newspaper," Mitchell recalled. "I sent Sonny up there alone.

"Marty Marshall is a clown. In the second round, Sonny hit him and could have knocked him out then. But Sonny tells me he was told to carry the boy three or four rounds so the fans could get their money's worth. Sonny got to laughing, Marshall hit him, and broke his jaw.

"When he came back to St. Louis, both jaws were swollen and fever had set in. The doctor wired his jaw. He was out of action for six months."

And Liston was "very angry" with Mitchell. "He voiced strong objection to my not going to Detroit when he got his jaw broke," Mitchell recalled. "He got very angry when I presented him a dentist's bill for $20. The operation cost the athletic commission $400!" This is Liston's version of the broken-jaw incident: "I was told to take it easy for a coupla rounds. Marshall's a clown—they told me—who'd bounce around and flick punches from all sides.

"I was standing there, kinda wondering, when all of a sudden he lets out a yell and with my mouth wide open, gaping, he slugged me right on the jaw. It didn't hurt but I couldn't close my mouth. I had to fight the last six rounds with my mouth open. After a while, it hurt bad."

And, in Detroit, where he—the modest father of a large family who worked as a stock checker for a paint company—Marty Marshall, brought to a pinnacle of fame he never knew as a fighter, told his version of his conquest of Liston prior to the Liston-Patterson title fight at Chicago:

"I beat him here in Detroit when I broke his jaw. A right cross. It's not true that I'd jumped in the air and whooped and that we were laughing it up all through the fight.

"I hit him. I didn't know his jaw was broken and I don't think he did, either. Not until the next day. But I got the decision."

It was while Liston was laying off, recovering from the broken jaw, that he became an unbearable financial burden to Mitchell and Harrison. As Mitchell related:

"Monroe Harrison had a large family. He didn't have the finances to come up with his part of the deal. It was hard to keep Sonny in a job after it got out that he was an ex-con. *That stigma.* It was all on me. I needed some help. I bought Harrison out for $600 and, in turn, sold his share to Eddie Yawitz, a St. Louis druggist."

Harrison's version is somewhat different:

"On January 13, 1955, my wife contracted meningitis and was hospitalized. What with the hospital bills, plus the loss of her income, I couldn't keep up my end. In February, 1955, I sold my half interest to Eddie Yawitz for $600—in Yawitz's drug store. I deposited most of the money in the Bank of St. Louis."

Harrison's version was detailed in an affidavit dated October 26, 1960, signed "in the presence of Detective Sergeant Joseph Moore and Detective George J. Nintemann and Robert L. Turley, investigator for the U.S. Senate Anti-Trust Committee."

Harrison, a one-time Joe Louis sparring partner and professional fighter who claims never to have been knocked off his feet is, today, as he's been for many years, custodian at the Carr Lane Branch School. He keeps a box of clippings and photographs in his basement "office" at the school. A heavy-set, friendly man, he talks willingly, and effusively, about both his personal career and his associations with Liston.

Following recovery from the broken jaw, Liston decisioned Neil Welch in eight rounds at St. Louis on March 1, 1955. Then, on April 21, Marty Marshall came to St. Louis to fight Liston again and was knocked out in the sixth round. But, Marshall has claimed, and the records show, that he knocked Liston down in this bout.

Now, throughout the rampant reams of publicity and newspaper stories written about Liston prior to his meeting with Patterson, it was said, as Liston said, that he'd never been knocked off his feet.

70

These reports caused Marshall to protest. During an interview with George Puscas of the *Detroit Free Press*, Marshall insisted that he had knocked Liston down in their rematch and the story gained national currency. However, Marshall's story exerted the impact of Liston's claim of never having been knocked off his feet. In fairness to Sonny, as we shall see, he had a witness who would testify that he was telling the truth.

But, back to Marshall:

"He hit me like no man should be hit," Marty told Puscas.

"He hit me so hard it didn't knock me out. It didn't even knock me down.

"But it hurt so much, I went down anyway.

"He's tough. That's one thing nobody can deny about that man. He hurts. *He hurts when he breathes on you.*

"But, I just can't understand why he insists he was never knocked down. I remember every little thing about it I wish it had never happened."

Marshall continued:

"It was the rematch in St. Louis . . . where I knocked him down. I just don't know why he wouldn't remember that.

"It was the fourth round. I knew I had to stay away from him, because if he hits you . . . man. *Patterson will find that out, too.*

"But Liston has a fault. He drags that right hand. I mean, he carries it too low. He came in with that left of his and I crossed over with my right to his jaw.

"He went down. I don't know whether he was down for an eight count because he needed it, or because the rules required it. But he was down.

"I'm sorry to this day about that. Man, am I sorry.

"He hit me after that like . . . nobody should be hit like that. I think about it now and I hurt.

"He came after me in the fifth round. He hit me with a right hand on my ear. It didn't knock me out and it didn't knock me down. But it hurt so much, I just had to go down anyway.

"The next round, he knocked me down three times. *I've got two parts of me that remember Sonny Liston—that ear he hit, and my stomach.*

"He hit me in the stomach with a left hand in the sixth. That wasn't a knockdown, either. It couldn't be. *I was paralyzed.* I just couldn't move. I couldn't move enough to fall down.

"But he didn't know I was hurt, because I was doubled over and his head was above me. He couldn't see my face to know I was in pain.

"It didn't matter. He knocked me down three times later in the round and that was it.

"I fought him again in 1956 and I just knew I couldn't let him touch me. He never hurt me that time, but he got a decision in ten rounds.

"But the thing that gets me is his not remembering the time I knocked him down. Everybody remembers. It was in the papers."

Small reward for a glorious survival!

But, Tony Anderson disputed Marshall when I asked him about "the knockdown."

Tony said:

"Sonny was no more knocked down by Marty Marshall than you are knocked down." I was sitting in a chair at the time. "Marshall landed a punch on Sonny's glove and Sonny had his feet so tied up he fell. The referee started to count. I told him then it wasn't a knockdown."

In between his second and third bouts with Marty Marshall, the third one fought at Pittsburgh, Pennsylvania on March 6, 1956, Liston kayoed Emil Brtko in five rounds at Pittsburgh on May 5, 1955; kayoed Calvin Butler in two rounds at St. Louis on May 25; kayoed Johnny Gray in six rounds at Indianapolis on September 13;

and kayoed Larry Watson in four rounds at East St. Louis on December 13, 1955.

They say that when Sonny has a fight scheduled, he's all business. But when he goes for a long period of time without having a fight to train for, he gets restless. According to Mitchell:

"After the bout with Brtko, a coal miner up from the hills of Pennsylvania, we began having problems getting opponents. We always had a problem getting sparring partners. Nobody wanted to spar. Sonny was too tough."

The record shows that Liston fought Butler twenty days after Brtko but did not fight between May 25 and September 13, 1955. After knocking out Gray on September 13, it was three months before he fought again—Watson on December 13. Then Liston fought no more until he met Marshall at Pittsburgh, still another three months, roughly.

The wheels of trouble had already started grinding.

The big excuse, or "out," Cus D'Amato, Patterson's manager, had for not fighting Liston after Liston rose to the position of No. 1 and most-logical challenger for the world's heavyweight title was his "underworld connections" or "bad associations." D'Amato—in one sense a magical manager, in another thought the best "mother" a fighter ever had—issued ultimatums that Liston had to make a break with these people before he could be even remotely considered for a title shot, and Patterson, until Liston dented his pride with words, backed D'Amato to the limit. The New York State Athletic Commission refused to sanction the Liston-Patterson title bout for New York City on much the same grounds and certain reputable elements in Chicago—where, believe it or not, the Joe Louis-Jim Braddock bout had been frowned on—launched a futile campaign to keep it out of the "Windy City."

The story of how control of Liston slipped out of Frank Mitchell's hands into "other hands" is one not even Senator Estes Kefauver's Senate Committee has completely documented, largely because, when they called the involved parties to testify, they conveniently took the Fifth Amendment.

John Vitale of St. Louis, is by all published accounts, a "bad man." The words "police record," "hoodlum," "gangster" are liberally sprinkled throughout stories of his associations with Liston. He apparently came into the picture during that period Mitchell mentioned, when it was difficult to secure fights for Liston.

In his office at the *St. Louis Argus*, when I interviewed him in October, 1962, Mitchell said this:

"I'm no associate of Vitale. I know him just as everybody else in St. Louis knows him. I met him on a golf course in a foursome—not by invitation. He was introduced to me. I, of all people, couldn't afford to discriminate. I learned that he was interested in boxing and boxers. I told him about Sonny and my hardships. Vitale said he'd give Sonny and another of my fighters, Jesse Bowdry, jobs at his concrete manufacturing company, at $65 a week. This was good money. This was my association with Vitale. I don't think I did anything wrong. I had to get him (Sonny) out of my pocket."

But—or, perhaps, *meanwhile*—when Mitchell accompanied Liston to Pittsburgh for the third fight with Marty Marshall, he met Tom Tannas, who had been associated with Jake Mintz in the management of Ezzard Charles, who succeeded Joe Louis as world's heavyweight champion by beating Jersey Joe Walcott in Chicago.

"I approached Tannas," Mitchell recalled, "and I told him, 'I've got the next heavyweight champion of the world. Can you move him for me?' Tannas agreed to take half. We signed a contract. This is, presumably, half of Mitchell's half—Yawitz seems mysteriously to have faded out of the picture, insofar as this account goes. Soon as Liston got back from the Marty Marshall bout in Pittsburgh, he had this trouble with the police department.

"I was in the middle. I was asking the police for leniency. The police were asking for cooperation. *Sonny told me this cop called him a black son of a bitch.* He said the cop said, 'Take care of your own business or I'll lock you up.' *The truth of the matter is, the police man had been drinking.* When the cop called him this name, Sonny just grabbed him, hugged him, took the pistol away from him and the cop fell on his leg and broke it. *He'd been in the hospital before because of his leg.* Sonny got excited. Not knowing what to do, he ran. He went to his sister's. *I was out of town.* They went down and picked Sonny up. The sentence sent him back again. He got off with nine months, did about seven. When the news broke in the papers, Tannas pulled out."

A St. Louis policeman was found unconscious in an alley, his leg broken, his face battered and his badge and club missing. The fighter was convicted as his assailant, but the original charges of assault with intent to kill and robbery were reduced, through the influence of racketeers, to assault and resisting arrest. He was sentenced to nine months. While awaiting trial in this case, he was arrested seven times on various other charges.
—Dan Parker, the famed New York sports writer, in a magazine article.

CHAPTER IX

Just what happened, really, in that St. Louis alley the night Sonny Liston allegedly assaulted that cop, took his gun away, and broke his leg, God in Heaven only knows.

But this conclusion can be drawn for sure:

This rap, more than any other, was to plague Sonny Liston worse than leprosy and was to turn law enforcement officers, *and boxing*, traditionally a refuge for un seemly characters, against him.

There are policemen in St. Louis—white and Negro—who seed their conversations about Liston with pure, unadulterated hate.

Dozens of writers, not necessarily to be blamed, have held this charge—cop-beating!—more religiously, more devastatingly, against Sonny than anything else he's ever done.

He beat a cop! Jesus!

It happened on the night of May 5, 1956. Sonny has said that he and Geraldine were attending a party at a friend's home and when she grew weary at a late hour, he called a cab.

About the time the Liston cab would have arrived, Patrolman Thomas Mellow reports:

"I was making my relief corner and passed an alley. A cab was parked in it with the parking lights on. From the entrance to the alley, I asked who the driver was. The driver came down, said his name was Patterson. I told him he could get a ticket, but I was going to let him move the cab.

"Then Liston came down.

" 'You can't give him no ticket,' he said, real rough like. The hell I can't,' I said. I took out my ticket book, flashlight, to get the city sticker number off the cab. As I started over, Liston came over and gave me a bear hug from the front, lifting me clear off the ground." Mellow said Liston and Patterson dragged him to the rear of the alley where, Mellow claimed, Liston took his gun.

Continuing his narrative, Mellow quoted Patterson as telling Liston to "shoot the white son of a bitch."

Mellow said, "Liston releases me and points the gun at my head. I'm pushing up on the barrel with both hands to keep from looking down the muzzle. They were walking all over me. I hollered, 'Don't shoot me.' Liston let up and then he hit me over the eye—with either his fist or the gun. Then they ran up the alley."

Now, this is Liston's version of the incident:

"I saw the cab pull up into the alleyway, and I hurried out of the house. Meanwhile, a cop came up and told the cabbie he was going to give him a ticket. I said, 'How come you going to give the cab a ticket? He's just doing his business.'

"The cop turns on me and says, 'You're a smart nigger, and when I say, 'I'm not smart,' he reaches for his gun and tries to take it out of his holster, but I take it away from him. Later, the cop said I was drunk. Now, how could a drunk handle a sober cop trained to make arrests and to pull his gun?"

Suffering a seven-stitch gash over his left eye and a smashed knee, Mellow was hospitalized.

Neither Mellow nor Liston talk freely about the "cop beating" incident today. Numerous versions of "what happened" have been published and there is startling variance in detail. For example: Geraldine is variously identified as "Geraldine Clark, thirty-one," "Geraldine Chambers," and "Mrs. Geraldine Liston." Liston has said that, in addition to insulting his race, Mellow also insulted his wife. Mitchell has said Liston told him Mellow called Sonny "a black son of a bitch." Mitchell also has said that Mellow's own record as a policeman was far from being exemplary, a charge supported by others in St. Louis, one of whom noted that "cops drink, too." Charges that Liston was drunk at the time were quickly dismissed by his friends. "He gets as sick as a dog . . .," one friend said. "Whatever happened in that alley, it wasn't Liston's drinking that caused it."

Mitchell's version of the incident reveals other elements of mystery. During an interview with the author, while including his own participation in the controversy, Mitchell said:

". . . I was in the middle . . . I was asking for leniency. The police were asking for cooperation. Sonny told me the cop called him a black son of a bitch and said "take care of your own business or I'll lock you up." The truth of the matter is, the policeman had been drinking.

"When the cop called him this name, Sonny just grabbed him, hugged him, took the pistol away from him and the cop fell on his leg and broke it. He'd been in the hospital before because of his leg.

"Sonny got excited. Not knowing what to do, he ran. He went to his sister's house.

"*I was out of town.* They went down and picked Sonny up. The sentence sent him back again. He got off with nine months and did about seven. When the news broke in the papers, Tannas pulled out."

Noting the inconsistencies of stories about "what actually happened that night," the *Saturday Evening Post* of August 13, 1960, gave this version of the Liston Mellow fracas:

"The official St. Louis police report, assembled by a special crew of investigating officers, states that Policeman Thomas Mellow saw a taxicab parked illegally in an alley, went to the house adjacent to the alley and asked if the driver was there. In the house were the cab driver, Liston and two women—one of them Geraldine Chambers, who is now Sonny's wife. The police report states that all four, and especially Liston, appeared to have been drinking. The report goes on to say that when the officer asked that the car be moved, Liston argued and began grappling with him. The others tried to separate them, but Liston and Policeman Mellow finally went outside to the alley. Later Mellow was found lying in the alley, badly beaten, with his uniform torn, his badge ripped off, and his revolver missing. When the police arrested Liston, Sonny admitted fighting with the officer and also told them where the gun was. He said he had taken it away in self-defense, because "the man was looking for trouble."

"Certain questions about this account have never been answered—why the officer didn't merely tag the illegally parked taxi; why he went into the house instead of just stating his business at the door. The report that Liston had been drinking also raised eyebrows. Whatever his faults, Sonny had never been known as a drinker; he always said he hated the taste of the stuff."

The January 29, 1957, issue of the *St. Louis Globe Democrat* reported that Charles (Sonny) Liston, twenty-four-year-old professional boxer, was sentenced to nine months in the City Workhouse by Circuit Judge David J. Murphy "yesterday" on his plea of guilty to an assault charge.

"Mellow, forty-one, suffered head injuries and a broken leg in a scuffle in an alley in the rear of the 2800 block of North Taylor Avenue," the *Globe-Democrat* said. "Mellow's revolver was stolen in the fracas, which started when he allegedly threatened to ticket an illegally parked taxicab operated by Willie Patterson, twenty-seven, of the 4000 block of Maffitt Avenue."

According to this report, Mellow claimed that Liston and Patterson dragged him into an alley and beat him when he threatened to ticket the cab. Mellow was left unconscious behind 2818 North Taylor Avenue. Mellow was hospitalized twice. Both Liston and Patterson denied the charge.

The story went on to say that a Miss Geraldine *Clark*, thirty-one, said she watched from the porch of the building as Liston argued with Mellow and then started to struggle with him. She said Patterson tried to separate them before the three men disappeared into the alley. Then she heard a cry from the alley: "Don't hurt me!" Minutes later, she saw Liston and Patterson emerge from the alley and make arrangements to leave in Patterson's cab.

Now the story takes another interesting turn:

Patterson *denied* participation in the assault. Police quoted him as saying he waited at the entrance to the alley and when Liston came out, they drove to the 15th Street home of a Liston relative. En route, Patterson told police, Liston displayed a .38 caliber revolver and said he had taken it from the officer. The gun was recovered at this address!

Examine this thing . . . turn it upside down, inside out, analyze it . . . and what have you got? Simply ... a mess! Any way you look at it, it's a mess.

It is another less-than-clear-cut incident in the life of Sonny Liston—and an objective analysis wedges a sizable hole of speculation through which doubt scores a point.

In St. Louis, a city not noted for racial equality at the time, a Southern-born Negro with a prison record, said to be illiterate or semi-illiterate, allegedly beats a cop, causes him to suffer a broken leg, takes his gun away and runs . . . and, yet, he draws no more than a nine-month sentence in the City Workhouse! How come he didn't draw fifty years in the pen—if he was guilty as charged? If the explanation is . . . "he had pull" . . . then, what does this mean, and where did he get it from, from whom, through whom? . . . Why, after making statements which sifted down to the charge of assault against Liston did Mellow clam up? What about reports that yet persist to this effect: Mellow, himself, was not an ideal policeman? Certainly, if he called Liston a black son of a bitch, or in another way hurled a racial epithet at him, Mellow was stepping way outside the boundaries of proper police methods and he was, as Liston said, certainly "looking for trouble." The questions asked by the *Saturday Evening Post* writer were pertinent. If the cab was illegally parked, why didn't Mellow merely stick a ticket on it, as policemen do in such cases thousands of times daily across the nation, and be on his way? Why did Mellow venture into the house, if he did indeed enter? What about Patterson's story?

Perhaps there is still one more question to be asked: Are some people arrest-prone, as others are accident prone?

Liston was arrested in May, 1956, on the cop-assault charge. He was tried in December, same year. *Meanwhile, he was arrested four times!*

On June 14, 1956, he was arrested for speeding. A week later, he was picked up as a suspected thief and was released. On August 14, he was arrested for failure to answer a summons. And, again on October 14, he was arrested as a suspected thief and was released.

"These are charges that most lawyers consider 'spitting on the sidewalk,'" Pete Hamill wrote in the *New York Post*, "but a pattern was beginning. The St. Louis police force apparently had declared war on Sonny Liston, and, in 1957, after Liston completed his nine-month sentence in the City Workhouse, they opened up with all their resources."

A friend of Liston's has said, "If it hadn't of been a cop (whom Liston was accused of beating), he'd never had that arrest record . . . I was under the impression in this country you're innocent until they prove you're guilty. So he was arrested a lot of times, but that doesn't mean he was guilty. You could be arrested tonight for murder. Does that mean you killed someone? They were harassing him because he hit a cop. Nobody ever mentions that maybe the cop deserved hitting."

Liston has admitted that St. Louis police picked him up "fifty or a hundred" times. "There was nothing they didn't pick me up for. If I was to go into a store and ask for a stick of gum, they'd say it was a stick-up."

"Every time he'd step out on the street, the police harassed him," Mitchell said. "They told him they were looking for 'an excuse to blow your brains out.' They told him that one day his body would be found in the river." The fact is, a St. Louis sports writer himself once told Liston that "some night you'll wind up dead." When the sports writer recalled this conversation later, he also remembered Liston's lack of reaction: "It didn't seem to move him at all."

In his *Chicago Sun-Times* story, Ray Brennan added this twist:

"*Mitchell* had a record of twenty-six St. Louis arrests, and the police disliked him intensely. It is possible that some of the police aversion rubbed off on Liston, as he now claims." Most of Mitchell's arrests involved gambling charges. But, it should be pointed out, Mitchell had handled other fighters—including Jimmy Fields, Jesse Bowdry, Fineda Cox, and Charley Riley ["I skyrocketed him right to the top"]—and none of these seemed to have engendered the kind of police enmity that Liston received.

St. Louis police have explained that they arrested Liston frequently "for a reason . . . we wanted to break up Liston's associations with hoodlums. Every time we could jump Liston up, find him, we did."

In the January 19, 1960, issue of the *St. Louis Post Dispatch*, Theodore C. Link wrote a story which now sheds more light on "Liston's associations." At the time, Link was reporting testimony heard by Senator Kefauver's Committee, including facets of Liston's tie-up with Blinky Palermo in Philadelphia, Pennsylvania.

(It was to become obvious that Liston's career was dead in St. Louis. His subsequent move to Philadelphia will be detailed in the next chapter. But Link's story is pertinent here.)

"Liston left St. Louis two years ago at the height of a nationwide investigation of boxing," Link wrote. "The St. Louis phase of the inquiry was conducted by police and agents of the FBI.

"Detectives arrested the burly boxer for questioning at that time because of his association with John J. Vitale, gangster and Mafia member; the late Raymond Sarkis, union business agent for whom he was reported to have served as a paid 'muscle man,' and with Robert (Barney) Baker, former boxer and Teamster's Union trouble shooter, who was cautioned by police to stay out of St. Louis.

"Liston contended he was being harassed by police because he had a prison record. He moved into quarters above a restaurant in

Philadelphia. Liston receives rent, food, clothing and use of an automobile at Palermo's expense, the *Post-Dispatch* learned.

"The boxer was reported to have admitted the existence of the arrangement to police, who talked with him on a visit here. Documentary evidence of the payment of Liston's expenses by Palermo was obtained when Palermo was arrested here for interrogation at the Akins-Martinez fight in June, 1958, at the arena.

"Palermo's briefcase contained receipts for three hundred dollars paid to the restaurant for Liston. Other receipts showed that Palermo paid Liston's bill at a hotel in 1958.

"Liston was in Chicago for a fight with Julio Mederos, Cuban boxer, whom he knocked out (May 14, 1958). Police learned that Vitale drove Liston to Chicago prior to the fight and turned the boxer over to Joe (Pep) Barone, Allentown (Pa.) matchmaker, who is reported to own an interest in Liston.

"Frank W. Mitchell, publisher of the *St. Louis Argus*, told this reporter he has a 12½ percent interest in Liston. Mitchell, a golfing companion of Vitale, denied that Vitale, Palermo and Frankie Carbo, an underworld figure now in prison, have financial interests in the fighter. Mitchell insisted that Barone is the principal owner of Liston.

"Barone, known in Pennsylvania boxing circles as an associate of Palermo, operates the Pep Athletic Club in Allentown . . .

"Liston told police two years ago that 'ownership' of him was divided among a number of individuals, whom he declined to name . . ."

While telling his own life story in the *Chicago American* five days before he fought Patterson, Liston said:

"People say to me, 'Well, (Joe) Louis and Patterson ran into the same problems but never were in real trouble like you have been. How do you explain that?'

"My answer is that, in the first place, I probably came from a worse environment than they did. They were raised in the North, in Detroit and New York, where people are at least aware of the juvenile problem.

"I was raised in the South, which is just now tackling the problem. So I was strictly on my own, running around without any kind of supervision. I am sure I would have been better had I been fortunate enough to meet a (John) Roxborough, (Julian) Black (Louis' managers), or D'Amato.

"Perhaps I would have been better had I come under the influence of such Catholic priests as Fathers Stevens, Charles Dismas Clark, and Edward Murphy of St. Ignatius Loyola Church in Denver. Father Murphy has been a great help to me lately. Before that, Father Dismas of St. Louis helped me, after Father Stevens first took an interest in me.

"You know what I often wonder about? Where were all these people who claim they are interested in juvenile delinquents when I was coming along as a kid?

"I looked for them, but never found them. I knew I needed some kind of adult help or advice, but they weren't around. Louis and Patterson found them at just the right time. I wish I'd been so lucky."

When Liston became embroiled in the cop-beating incident, he was suspended from boxing by the Missouri State Athletic Commissioner, Charles W. Pian. When Liston came out of the City Workhouse, St. Louis police were opposed to resumption of his boxing career. "Every time he fights," a policeman explained, "half the hoodlums in the country turn up in St. Louis." Captain John A. Doherty, a nationally reputed lawman, liked boxing but he disliked hoodlums more. His orders to his men were: "Arrest all known gangsters on sight. If they don't belong in St. Louis and if you haven't got anything on them, run them out of town."

Officers dressed in plain clothes were stationed throughout the arena whenever Liston fought in St. Louis.

But although the police thought Liston should not be permitted to resume fighting, Pian thought he was entitled to another chance.

"After the series of arrests," Pian has recalled, "Liston came to me and asked for another chance. I talked to Captain John A. Doherty, then head of the hoodlum squad, and to several sports writers and they agreed he might merit another chance, if gotten away from hoodlums..."

Pian obtained approval for the lifting of Liston's boxing suspension. But this was not tantamount to the immediate re-launching of Liston's career.

"You couldn't get any fighter to come here," Pian has explained, "knowing that the police would be watching every move."

On January 29, 1958, Liston resumed his career in Chicago, where he knocked out Billy Hunter in the second round. On March 11, he returned to Chicago and kayoed Ben Wise in the fourth round. On April 3, he decisioned Bert Whitehurst in ten rounds in St. Louis.

Then he moved to Philadelphia. He'd somehow come under new management. But his troubles weren't over.

"Kefauver warned Liston to 'shake off' racketeers John J. Vitale, Frank (Blinky) Palermo and other leeches if he wants a crack at the title. Otherwise . . . 'You may not be able to fight anywhere.' Liston admitted ties over the years with Vitale and Palermo. But he argued in effect he had little choice about his associates in the boxing trade if he wanted to get ahead. 'What was I to do, starve to death?' "
—Edward W. O'Brien, in the *St. Louis Globe Democrat*, December 14, 1960.

"Sonny Liston, the 'Fighter with a Past' . . . is what they call the heavyweight champion in Philadelphia."
—Malcolm Poindexter, Philadelphia writer for this book.

CHAPTER X

A man would have better luck trying to find his way through the Mammoth Cave blind-folded than he would while attempting to unravel the mystery of Sonny Liston's changing management from early 1958 to mid-1962. The problem of management became a touchy thing with Liston himself after he set serious chase to then-champion Floyd Patterson and found himself blocked because of, or on the excuse of, his "associations." Exasperated at one point, Liston said, "I've got to get myself a manager who isn't hot—one like Kefauver!"

It has been reported that, early in 1958, a reputable Chicago businessman who "dabbled in the fight game as a hobby," told Mitchell, "I think I can get some fights here for Sonny. We might even line up a television sponsor on a local or regional basis." A three-year contract was drawn on February 5, 1958, according to this report, and it was agreed that Sonny would receive fifty percent of his purses while Mitchell and the Chicagoan would share the other half and pay expenses. [This report obviously omits Eddie Yawitz as a participant.] The contract was signed a week after Liston knocked out Billy Hunter. Shortly after Liston knocked out Ben Wise—March 11, 1958—this contract became inoperative.

That is, the arrangement between Mitchell and the Chicagoan had no more effect.

The St. Louis attorney who drew up the contract has said, "It (was) a completely legal contract. So far as I knew then, it supplanted any previous arrangement which Mitchell held and was the only one in existence."

After Liston had moved to Philadelphia, the Chicagoan was asked, "Are you in the picture anymore?"

The Chicagoan replied negatively, explaining: "Some of the boys in the fight mob came up to me one night and said they were taking Sonny East."

When Mitchell was asked for an explanation, he said:

"We weren't getting any place. Sonny could go on knocking out those ham-and-eggers forever and nobody would notice him. I knew that Sonny was good enough to beat any heavyweight in the country, but it looked like we were never going to get the big chance. At one of those Chicago fights, I saw Blinky Palermo. He asked me the same question I had been asking myself: 'Why waste Liston when he was ready for the big time?' "

"Frank (Blinky) Palermo, a former fight manager with a lengthy police record, has been barred by boxing commissions in many states," the August 13, 1960, *Saturday Evening Post* article said, "but he is still *considered* a dominant behind-the-scenes figure. Palermo is a good friend of John Vitale, the so-called 'No. 1 hoodlum' of St. Louis, who . . . was already interested in Liston.

"The upshot of Palermo's conversation with Mitchell was that Liston moved to Philadelphia. Joseph (Pep) Barone—another friend of Blinky's—became Sonny's principal owner of record."

This same magazine article quoted Mitchell as saying, "I still have Liston under contract. I am entitled to 12½ percent for my share every time Sonny fights. Blinky doesn't own Sonny. When I told Blinky my troubles, he said he'd get Pep Barone to handle the fighter in Philadelphia."

When I interviewed Mitchell in St. Louis after Liston had won the title, he said:

"When I was in town (Chicago) for the Sugar Ray Robinson-Carmen Basilio fight (March 25, 1958), I saw Blinky Palermo. I told him, 'I've got the next heavy weight champion' . . . I had made the same statement to Joe Louis, Truman Gibson, Jr., (then an executive of the International Boxing Club), and Papa Dee in Detroit.

"Blinky said, 'I can't manage him, but I can get somebody to help you.'

"When I got back to St. Louis, I got a long-distance call from Pep Barone. He said, 'I understand you have a fighter you want some help with.'

"Yes. I do. I referred him to ————"—Mitchell mentioned the name of a Chicagoan—"and told him I was going back to Chicago for a fight." The idea was that Mitchell would talk to Barone at the Chicago fight. Liston fought Julio Mederos there on May 14, 1958, knocking him out in the third round.

Mitchell continued, "I was unloading my stable of fighters, devoting more attention to the paper. The police were harassing Liston. He wasn't doing anything. He knew better. He was clean. The only thing, being ignorant, the only people he knew were in the ghetto and he'd go down there to visit his sister and the police would pick him up.

"I went back to Chicago and met Barone. Barone said he was taking the fighter over and taking him to Philadelphia."

"I asked Sonny, 'Is this okay?' Sonny said, 'Yes. I want to leave St. Louis. The police are bothering me.'"

Mitchell told me, "I assumed they'd gotten in touch with ———"—he mentioned the Chicagoan again. "Barone said when Sonny was made, I'd be 'in.'

"Liston has never made anything big yet. The income tax people don't seem to believe my story. They come around and ask, 'How could you give this golden boy away?'"

Mitchell said that from "then on," Barone took over. He said he was "practically out of the picture." He said he didn't know what Palermo did—"I imagine he helped him in some way." Mitchell said, "Liston has promised to take care of me, but he hasn't. He still owes me two thousand dollars—what I invested. I had to pawn my jewelry to pay lawyer's fees when the trouble came up. Yet, I'm condemned for associating with hoodlums. I was subpoenaed by Kefauver. People ask, why did I take the Fifth [amendment]? Because I couldn't remember accurately the whole story. I was afraid I'd subject myself to perjury. So I took the Fifth."

At this time, I asked Mitchell: "What kind of a guy is Sonny Liston, really?"

"He's playful, jolly," Mitchell said. "He likes to kid all the time. He has a great sense of humor. But I think had he had an education, he wouldn't have been a professional man . . . To my knowledge, he doesn't drink . . . He got angry with me once—when I didn't go to Detroit that time he got his jaw broke . . . He was not a profane man at the time I had him . . . He's really good at heart. He likes children. He has a lot of sympathy for underprivileged people. His wife is his right arm. She reads to him, writes his letters. When he first came to me, he couldn't write his name. He had to draw it . . . When he first came to St. Louis, he ran with rough kids around Ninth and O'Fallon and Franklin, down in that area. It was just a beehive of activity in juvenile crime. It was a hell hole. It was a ghetto, a slum area . . . poor housing, wobbly steps, broken windows, filth! . . . I tried to get him to go to school—night school—but he wouldn't. I tried to teach him to write at the office—but he became impatient. It lasted about a week or so . . . Now—he's calling the shots. He has the final say. He can keep out of trouble if he gets the proper advisers. He needs a good publicity man . . ."

Liston's career began to gain momentum immediately after his new managerial situation was arranged.

In a nationally televised bout at Chicago on August 6, 1958, he knocked out Wayne Bethea in fifty-six seconds. Truman Gibson, Jr., said then he would offer Patterson two hundred and fifty thousand dollars to fight Sonny. The offer was ignored. Cus D'Amato was, at

90

that time, waging his celebrated "feud" with the International Boxing Club.

In a sense, it can be said that Liston's "chase" of Patterson began immediately after he kayoed Bethea—although, in its early phase, it was switched from Patterson to Ingemar Johansson and then back to Patterson, as Floyd was having troubles of his own.

Liston knocked out Frankie Daniels in the first round at Miami Beach on October 7, 1958; he decisioned Bert Whitehurst in ten rounds, and again at St. Louis, on October 24; and rounded out his fighting for the year with an eighth-round knockout of Ernie Cab at Miami Beach on November 18.

Liston fought four times in 1959, scoring knockouts over Mike DeJohn, Cleveland Williams, Nino Valdes, and Willi Besmanoff.

He fought DeJohn at Miami Beach on February 18 and knocked him out at 2:43 of the sixth round. Sonny weighed 209¼ pounds, DeJohn, 202. Employing a deft left jab to the face, Sonny piled up an early advantage, then opened up his assault in the fifth and sixth rounds, battering DeJohn's head and body with left hooks and right crosses.

In the sixth, DeJohn took the mandatory eight count. Liston drove him around the ring with a series of lefts and rights to the head. DeJohn was down for another count near the finish, before Referee Jimmy Peerless stopped the fight.

This victory brought Liston's record to twenty-two wins in twenty-three bouts, including thirteen knockouts. Afterward, Barone said:

"Now, we want only rated fighters. We want to fight the best and we feel public opinion will force a match with whoever is champion after Floyd Patterson fights Ingemar Johansson."

Liston has said repeatedly that Cleveland Williams is the hardest hitter in the ring. While he was preparing for the title fight with Patterson at Chicago, Sonny said that if he should win the championship, he would defend it against Williams (Shortly after Liston did win the title, a Texas millionaire bought Williams' contract!). But when Liston met Williams in Miami Beach on April

15, it was the same old routine—a three-round knockout! In Chicago on August 5, Liston knocked out Nino Valdes in the third round. Valdes' downfall began when Liston hit him in the stomach with a left. A left hook to the head staggered Valdes, who dropped his gloves. Liston smashed him to the floor with a right cross.

"The win over Valdes was one of two turning points in Sonny's career," Mitchell has said. "The other was his first victory over Johnny Summerlin back in 1954. Each man had a bigger reputation at the time than anyone Sonny had met before. Because he's big and strong, you don't realize unless you talk to him that he can be scared like anybody else. And he was scared going up against Summerlin and Valdes."

On December 9, Liston knocked out Willi Besmanoff. With blood pouring from cuts over Besmanoff's eyes, he failed to come out for the seventh round. Again Liston set up the victory in early rounds with his left jab, opened up a right-handed attack in the third, and finished his man with a two-handed, corner attack in the sixth.

Meanwhile, Liston had his first Philadelphia law brush in June. There was an auto accident, involving Liston and John Polite, then twenty-two. According to Patrolman David E. Knox, Liston and Polite were *fighting* when Knox arrived in answer to a radio call. The officer said that when he questioned Liston and Polite about the incident, they became loud and unruly. Liston claimed someone had slugged him from behind for calling "them" a name, but he said he didn't know who did it.

There was no arrest!

Sonny fought five times in 1960.

His victims—all but one knocked out—were Howard King, Cleveland Williams (again!), Roy Harris, Zora Folley, and Eddie Machen.

He knocked out King, a trial horse of a fighter, in the eighth round.

He improved his record on Williams by one round, scoring a knockout this time in the second.

Roy Harris, the one-time Texas schoolteacher, was a bigger name. He'd gained a title fight with Patterson at Los Angeles in 1958, had knocked Floyd down, and lasted into the twelfth round with him, before succumbing to a knockout.

Liston disposed of Harris in the first round. Harris was then ranked as the sixth best heavyweight in the world.

Out-weighing the Texan 212½ pounds to 195, Liston knocked Harris underneath the ropes for a nine count with a powerful left hook. As Harris arose, shaking his head, Liston knocked him down again. Harris took another nine count, staggered to his feet, only to be floored for the third time by a vicious left hook. The three knockdowns in a single round brought Liston an automatic technical knockout victory under National Boxing Association rules.

"He's a better puncher than Patterson," said Harris, who'd lost only two of his thirty-two fights.

Pep Barone said, "We want a title fight, of course, but we know that will take time. We'll fight Zora Folley, Eddie Machen, or anyone. In other words, we don't want to get rusty while waiting for that title fight."

On July 18, Liston kayoed Folley in the third round at Denver. He was now rated the No. 1 heavyweight championship challenger.

Machen, a spoiler whose magic had somehow or other left him the night he fought Ingemar Johansson abroad, entered his September 7 fight with Liston at Seattle obviously intending to go the distance. He went the distance, twelve rounds, in a dull bout which left Liston with contempt for his foe, though he won the decision.

In September, 1960, a story out of Washington announced that Liston had been summoned to a "ring inquiry." This inquiry was being conducted by Senator Estes Kefauver's Committee, and it was then that Kefauver warned Sonny to "shake off" racketeers Vitale, Palermo and other leeches if he wanted a crack at the title.

It was then that Liston argued that he had little choice about his associates in the boxing business and asked, "What was I to do, starve to death?"

Liston said that, as far as he knew, neither Vitale, Palermo, nor Carbo owned a piece of him.

Described by reporters as "an able witness," Liston said he had thirty thousand dollars in the bank and owned his home in Philadelphia. When Senate investigators tried to pin him down to specifics, however, Liston evaded them by saying, "I can't recall."

When he was questioned about his testimony before St. Louis detectives (Liston once told St. Louis Detective Lieutenant Frank Burns that he made occasional collect telephone calls to Vitale to find out "how everything was in St. Louis"), Liston said he told them "what they wanted me to say" just to be rid of "their constant harassment."

An outgrowth of this investigation was an "indication from evidence" that John Vitale owned twenty-four percent of Liston.

Robert Turley, a sub-committee investigator, said Frank Mitchell had admitted he'd been receiving twenty-five percent of the manager's share from Liston's purses, even though he (Mitchell) "supposedly bowed out as Liston's manager in 1958 in favor of Barone." Mitchell, as said, took the Fifth.

At one point during this hearing, when various underworld characters and alleged percentage owners of his contract were mentioned, Liston cracked: "I'd have to make a million dollars a month to take care of all these people."

Senator Everett M. Dirksen (Republican of Illinois) asked Liston why police kept picking him up.

"That's what I'd like to know," Sonny said. "They never told me anything. They just picked me up and put me in the can. Captain Doherty (St. Louis) he told me to my face that if I wanted to stay alive, I better leave St. Louis. He said otherwise they might find me in an alley."

Liston said that one time some former fighters in the St. Louis police department "wanted the Captain to let them take me down to the basement. I said, 'Okay—you guys think you're tough!' But the Captain didn't let them."

Senator Kefauver himself was to write a pre-title fight story involving Liston. Appearing in the *Family Weekly* of September 16, 1962, the story was entitled, *Will Gangsters Be the Real Winners?* This was speculation based on a Liston victory.

"As the September 25 heavyweight championship bout between Sonny Liston and Floyd Patterson approaches," Kefauver wrote, "those who know Liston's history are unhappy.

"The reason for their concern is an unanswered question: Does the underworld *still* control Liston?"

As matters now stand, no one can be sure whether Liston will keep all, or substantially all, of his purse—or whether it will go to racketeers.

"This doubt exists because there is no way to compel such disclosures. The only effective guarantee is provided in my Senate Bill 1474, the Federal Boxing Control Bill, which is pending in the Senate.

"In 1960 and 1961, the Senate Subcommittee on Anti-trust and Monopoly, of which I am chairman, held hearings which proved that boxing was monopolistically controlled by a group of criminals.

"Investigation revealed that the power structure was built like a pyramid. At the bottom, or the working level, were fighters like Liston. Above them were the legally listed managers, 'front men' chosen because of their relative freedom from criminal records. In the next tier of the hierarchy were the regional chiefs, such as Frank (Blinky) Palermo, who made most of the decisions for Liston and other mob-controlled fighters.

"At the very top was Frank Carbo, czar of professional boxing in America, now in Alcatraz. This able and evil man for years held absolute sway over professional boxing. He decided whether important bouts were to be held and secretly acted as manager for one or the other—or sometimes both—of the principals.

"Some persons have asked me if I was not being unduly harsh with Liston. I have nothing but good will toward this unfortunate man who, whatever his failings, came into our committee room, raised his right hand, and answered the questions put to him. Those who heard him that day must carry with them the haunting memory of the tragic story he told.

"One of twenty-five children in an Arkansas share cropper's family . . ."

"I am sorry that Sonny Liston's past record is not a good one, but I am concerned more about the future.

"Who controls the heavyweight contender today? The public has no way of knowing—and this is particularly important in the case of Liston because there is proof that he was the property of a group of racketeers controlled by Carbo. In 1958, when the time came to move Sonny upward, he was sent from St. Louis to Chicago. Frank Mitchell, his manager at the time, merely told him that Joseph (Pep) Barone would be his manager in the future. As Liston told it at the hearings:

" 'I went up to fight this fight, and Frank Mitchell told me when I left St. Louis that it would be a man by the name of Pep Barone to come up with the contract and for you to sign it and he will get you East where you can get sparring partners and more fights, a better trainer.'

"Liston signed to fight with Barone as manager March 11, 1958. After that, his star rose quickly. On May 14, his fight with Julio Mederos was nationally televised, and thereafter he appeared frequently on television.

"One does not begrudge him his increased earnings, but unfortunately not all the money went to him. [At another time, Liston had said that one of his Chicago purses amounted to $6,600 but that he received only $600!) One may look skeptically on the claim of St. Louis police that 'one of the top gangsters' in that city was sharing Liston's earnings, but there can be no doubt that Palermo was getting a share.

"At no time did Liston say that Palermo was his manager—and it is just possible that he did not know it . . ."

In this article, Kefauver cited evidence showing that on May 15, 1959, Truman Gibson's company had given Palermo a $5,000 check which Palermo cashed. The voucher stated: "Re: Services Liston."

Kefauver went on:

"Here is what was said when Gibson was questioned by counsel before the sub-committee:

"'Did you instruct the auditor or whoever made that designation to make this statement on the check requisition?'

" 'Yes, I did.'

" 'Was that $5,000 paid for the services of Sonny Liston?'

" 'It was paid for Palermo's, since I was paying him.'"

" 'Was it paid for Palermo's services in securing Sonny Liston for the IBC?'

" 'Yes."

The Palermo association was to hound Sonny Liston even after he'd won the world's heavyweight championship.

Meanwhile more trouble was brewing in Philadelphia.

After two arrests, the Commission surmised, Liston's actions were detrimental to boxing and the public. Liston waived a hearing and threw himself on the mercy of the commissioners.

—Malcolm Poindexter, for this book.

CHAPTER XI

Between September 7, 1960, and September 25, 1962, Sonny Liston only fought twice. On the earlier date, he decisioned Eddie Machen at Seattle. On the latter date, of course, he knocked Floyd Patterson out of the heavyweight throne room. The two bouts he fought between Machen and Patterson were knockout victories over Howard King at Miami Beach, Florida, on March 8, 1961 and Albert Westphal at Philadelphia, Pennsylvania, on December 4, 1961.

Sonny spent the interim getting in and out of difficulties with police and the Pennsylvania State Athletic Commission, chasing Patterson, changing managers and associates, in an effort to "cleanse" himself sufficiently to become acceptable to Cus D'Amato and Patterson and other boxing commissions; explaining his life's predicament to numerous magazine and newspaper writers who, obviously, found in him some of the liveliest copy of the ages, a situation which was a perfect set-up for a crusade (or, perhaps, a crucifixion); maintaining a good home-life, and, despite his various difficulties, yet without any calculated effort on his part, creating among neighbors the impression that he was "a nice man."

The Sonny Liston his Philadelphia neighbors saw every day, as their statements in the next chapter will show, was the absolute contradiction of the "character" police somehow or other frequently nabbed in their nets; Sonny Liston at, and around, home was the exact opposite of the image created by published reports of his record and personality. On the one hand is the Sonny Liston with a police record, presumably tough, mean, vicious, evil, destructive. On the other hand, we find a kindly gentleman. What is the bridge between this Dr. Jekyll and Mr. Hyde? In the foggy night one traverses as he attempts to "fix" the real Sonny Liston, the bridge begins to emerge in the distinctive outlines of ignorance (in the sense of making unwise associations, in the sense of wearing a chip on the shoulder, especially in dealings with police); restlessness-with-inactivity, a real drag for a man with, apparently, a minimum of constructive imagination and a minimum of stimulating advisers; a playful, practical-joking, nature that, while harmless most of the time, can be dangerous when left unshackled by an understanding of what is, and what isn't, considered proper by the bulk of society. Whatever Sonny Liston is, whatever he isn't, there seems to be little disputing a claim that society—indeed, where were all those benefactors of juvenile delinquents when he was growing up?—is so deeply involved in the manufacturing of this man, or personality, that society really is in no position to view him from an angle posed down the nose. Stop to consider just two facts: Although Liston has been characterized in the most horrible terms of humanity, still there is not to be found in any available research material a statement that says he was deliberately unsportsmanlike in a single fight; the same Sonny Liston who grew up in shocking poverty, in one of the most depressing areas, racially, in the nation, who came into a major city as an untutored stranger and was shunted to the worse sections of town, who had no mother to guide him during most of his residence in that city (Mrs. Helen Liston left St. Louis after a short stay, returned to Arkansas to make two crops, then went to live in Gary, Indiana), where he was sacked to the slums . . . this man still, according to everyone who knows him, has responded to the love and advice of his wife, has saved his money, has purchased a good home. Of course, none of this justifies all the charges made against Liston; perhaps nothing can. But it seems to be just too easy to find fault with him; the whole case against him, as expressed by most of his critics, seems just too pat for complete purchase. Make just a simple speculation and Liston's life, like baseball, comes out as just "a game of inches." Leave him right there in Forrest City, Arkansas, for birth. Then, suppose he'd gone to school with kids he knew, kids who knew him, at the proper age. Let's say that, while he perhaps would never have graduated *cum laude*, he would have discovered something of intellectual interest and, growing big and strong as he was, quite possibly would have discovered football and starred as a fullback or as a lineman. He would have needed no more to acquire an athletic scholarship. Since the indisputable fact is that Sonny grew big, strong, and agile, possessing a great deal of athletic ability, why can't Sonny Liston be placed, in speculation, as a current counterpart of Jimmy Brown; or, even, as a man who emerged from college, with an altogether different set of circumstances behind him, to work his way toward his present position, heavyweight champion of the world? *A critic may call this folly vs. fact. But, be it "folly," it still proves that Sonny Liston isn't solely responsible . . .*

Yet those who make a defense for Sonny Liston compose one of the nation's smallest minorities! When reporters interviewed Sonny after his early fights, they were unable to draw out of him much more than shrugs, grunts, or mumbles. Few of them realized, apparently, that Sonny was not then able to handle their barrages and retreated into a cold, steely shell in self-defense. Since Sonny was "poor copy" as a fighter, perhaps naturally, editorial attention was concentrated more heavily than it would otherwise have been on the facts of his brushes with the law—and, just as naturally, a man such as Liston, if not anyone, would resent this heavy concentration of interest on his "mistakes." Rocky Graziano, a once great fighter who more recently has been a weekly television performer, has been quoted as saying, "Compared to what I did, Sonny Liston is an angel." It is no secret that Archie Moore got off to a wrong start in life, but Archie, vastly more talkative and quicker to learn the facts of life [his early detainment brought immediate rehabilitation], has never suffered the out-prison punishment that has been, and still is being, meted out to Liston. At the same time that New York refused to sanction Liston for fighting in that state, another boxer with a prison record, Rubin Carter, was making his own climb toward a title bout in another division. But Carter, too, is a glib person—one whose difficulties with the law have been explained more on the basis of carelessness of

101

attitude rather than on inherent, or innate, or confirmed, no-goodness. Mitchell has said that he made a hundred, if not a thousand, mistakes in handling Liston. Liston might well have been guided through his off-fight hours far more wisely than he was, as other fighters have been guided and aided by publicists and protected. Even after he won the heavyweight title—the very night he did, in fact—there was evidence that Liston was not getting the proper "public relations" handling. Although hundreds of respectable citizens visit the place, and it's legalized, and it cannot be adjudged as being in anyway unlawful or "wrong" to go there, Liston miscued public relations-wise when he took in a show and ate post-title fight dinner at a famous club owned by a man who, not long before, had been the subject of attack because of his own police record. Generally, the press did not make anything of Liston's visit to the night club; but one segment noted it and wrote a story inferring that "birds of a feather flock together."

Not all newspapermen found joy in rendering judgments on Liston, of course. Three newsmen were involved in Liston's being paroled from Missouri State Penitentiary. After all of Liston's difficulties with the law, there always were reputable newsmen who saw good in him and argued on behalf of him. Most of the writers who have profiled him have devoted space to his good sides, although it has been much easier, probably natural, to view him as "boxing's angry man" and "the bad boy of boxing" than as something better. The influence of the news about Liston, leading up to his victory in the heavyweight title bout, worked heavily against him among the public. Even in the Missouri State Penitentiary, many Negro prisoners hoped that Patterson would win because they believed Liston, as champion, would be a discredit to their race. Manhattan NAACP President Percy Sutton spoke for these prisoners and many other Negroes when he said, prior to the title bout, "Hell, let's stop kidding. I'm for Patterson because he represents us better than Liston ever could or would . . ."

While Liston was in Seattle to fight Machen, notice of the filing of a ninety-thousand-dollar damage suit against him by St. Louis Patrolman Thomas Mellow was served. Ten days later, it was reported that Liston had filed a petition with County Clerk Norman

R. Riddell requesting removal of a ninety-thousand-dollar damage suit against him from state to federal court.

"Attached to the petition," said the *Seattle Post Intelligencer*, "filed by the boxer by his attorney, Philip L. Burton, was a copy of a King County Superior Court complaint, apparently not yet filed in Superior Court.

"The complaint was drawn by Seattle Attorney Arthur E. Piehler for Thomas Mellow, a Missouri policeman, who alleges his leg was broken by Liston on May 5, 1956, while Mellow was on duty.

"In his petition, Liston points out the suit should be transferred to United States District Court since the parties are residents of different states, Liston of Pennsylvania and Mellow of Missouri."

There has been no published report of a settlement of this suit.

On May 17, 1961, Liston was arrested in Philadelphia—his first there, no formal complaint was filed in the 1959 case—for corner lounging near his home. Patrolman James Best said he went to a corner to check on complaints about men congregating there. He said he found Liston and another man at the corner and asked them to move. He said Sonny refused and asked, "Why not arrest me?"

Best did.

Four hours later—at night—Liston was freed of the charge during a special hearing by Magistrate Harry Ellick, who commented: "I'm surprised that a man who has reached your pugilistic heights would get involved in anything so foolish as this."

Attorney Morton Witkin, Liston's representative in the case and also a man who had served as both majority and minority leader of the Pennsylvania House of Representatives, has presented this version of the incident:

"Sonny was signing autographs when the officer, James Best, who didn't recognize him, told him to move along. Sonny refused and was taken to the police station. There, the desk sergeant recognized him, heard his story and dismissed the incident as a misunderstanding. Sonny, *who can be strong-willed to a fault*, wanted a lift back. 'The red car brought me here,' he said. 'Let the red car take me back.' That was the remark they locked him up for."

On June 12, 1961, Liston was arrested in Philadelphia, Pennsylvania, on a more serious charge, and a probe of his dismissal in this case created still more sensationalism.

John Warburton, a Fairmount Park guard, said he was on patrol around 3 A.M. on June 12 when he saw two cars stopped beside each other on Lansdowne Drive, near Sweet Briar. Warburton said that when he approached, two men jumped into one of the cars and sped away with the lights out. The driver of the other car was a woman who said the men had pulled her over and pretended to be officers.

It was charged that Liston had impersonated an officer. Isaac Cooper, who had been riding with Liston, was named a co-defendant. Both were cleared of the charges by Magistrate E. David Keiser, who said that Liston and Brown had been guilty only of errors of judgment when they halted Mrs. Dolores Ellis as she drove through a lonely stretch of the park. Liston and the co-defendant were ordered to apologize to Mrs. Ellis in the court, and did.

In court, Mrs. Ellis testified that she had stopped her car when Liston's automobile pulled alongside. She said a spotlight was shone in her face and she was twice ordered to get out. She said she remained in her car and Liston remained in his. In reporting the incident, police said the two men had run back to their car when Warburton approached. Richard Edwards, a detective who entered the investigation after the arrests, said Liston had told him he thought he knew Mrs. Ellis and that was why he stopped her car. George Katz, then Liston's manager-of-record, testified that Liston was doing road work in the park and that Cooper was accompanying him. Charges of disorderly conduct and resisting arrest, also brought against Liston and his co-defendant at the time, were likewise dismissed.

The Pennsylvania State Athletic Commission had said that Liston's boxing license would be suspended if he were convicted of the charges involved in the Ellis case. The District Attorney's office launched an investigation of the June 12 arrest and subsequent dismissal. On July 14, 1961, Liston's license was suspended indefinitely.

After two arrests, the Commission now surmised, Liston's actions were "detrimental to boxing and the public."

Liston waived a hearing and threw himself on the mercy of the commissioners.

Commissioners James H. Crowley, Alfred M. Klein, and Paul Sullivan deliberated nearly an hour and then announced their verdict to seventy-five people crowded into the small State Building office.

The suspension took effect in all member states of the National Boxing Association and, of course, destroyed temporarily Liston's rating as the No. 1 heavyweight title challenger.

"The Commission is very dismayed and chagrined at your conduct since we granted you your license to box in Pennsylvania," Klein told Liston. "You disregarded (our) warning and again got yourself engaged with the law."

He continued:

"The Commission has decided unanimously to impose upon you an indefinite suspension until such time as you have rehabilitated yourself and demonstrated a respect for the law. When you can come in and prove that, and we find you deserving, we will reinstate you." Commissioner Sullivan observed that Liston had great physical and moral potential. He said the Commission didn't want to blight the boxer's career.

Liston replied in a brief typewritten statement, saying: "I regret that I have caused the Pennsylvania State Athletic Commission any embarrassment by reason of my indiscreet behavior. I can assure the Commission that from now on in, I shall so conduct myself as to creditably merit the confidence you have imposed on me by granting me a boxer's license. I place myself in your hands."

News that the District Attorney's office was investigating this case broke on July 12, two days prior to Liston's suspension by the Pennsylvania State Athletic Commission.

Assistant District Attorney Paul M. Chalfin said a complete investigation was being made to see if a re-arrest was warranted. Chalfin, who had already questioned Isaac Cooper and Warburton, said that no representative of the District Attorney's office had been on hand when the charges were dropped.

In the *New York Mirror* of Friday, July 14, the renowned sports writer Dan Parker wrote:

"George Katz has spoken. So have Magistrates E. David Keiser and Harry J. Ellick. But it seems the final word hasn't been uttered yet in the remarkable case of Sonny Liston, the 3 A.M. road-worker and notorious jail bird whom the Philadelphia magistrates treat as a Man of Distinction.

"Sonny is the No. 1 heavyweight contender who, in recent weeks, wiggled out of two entanglements with the law. Katz manages 10 percent of Sonny who Blinky Palermo, Philadelphia hoodlum, piloted until the so-called sale of his contract to Pep Barone who, in turn, was supposed to have peddled it to Liston himself for a reported seventy-five thousand dollars. Magistrate Keiser is the distinguished jurist who in dismissing charges against Liston of failure to move off when ordered by a cop, resisting a police officer, conspiracy, resisting arrest, disorderly conduct and shutting off the lights of his car to avoid arrest, lumped all these counts into a four-word phrase—'an error of judgment.'

"This phrase could also be used to describe Magistrate Keiser's action in hearing the case against Liston at 8:30 A.M. instead of waiting for the regular court session to open at 9 A.M. as called for. It could be, of course, that the kindly magistrate wanted to let Sonny do his roadwork before the sun got too high in the sky, and certainly with no intention of dismissing the defendant before an observer from the District Attorney's staff arrived to case the hearing for his chief . . .

"District Attorney James C. Crumlish ordered an investigation, with special emphasis on Magistrate Keiser's reason for holding his hearing . . . at 8:30 A.M., a half-hour before it was supposed to be called, with a special representative of the District Attorney in attendance. When this official arrived at 9 A.M., the hearing was over and Liston was probably being measured for a set of wings and a halo to match 'the dawn of a new era' which loquacious Mr. Katz had announced Sonny was about to start . . .

"One story being circulated in Philadelphia fight circles is that the woman in the case was "squared' through payment of $2,500 to her lawyer. Officially, she agreed to withdraw her charge after Liston apologized for 'his mistake' . . ."

A Philadelphia reporter informed Jet magazine that District Attorney, James C. Crumlish, Jr., is investigating a report that the fix of five thousand dollars was arranged so that heavyweight contender Charles (Sonny) Liston could be freed on charges of resisting arrest in Fairmount Park.

"Crumlish received a letter from an unidentified tipster that the five-thousand-dollar payoff was split two ways. The letter was postmarked Camden, New Jersey . . .

The District Attorney has ordered the re-arrest of Liston and Isaac Cooper . . .

"Among those to be questioned by Assistant District Attorney Paul Chalfin are Mrs. Ellis, her attorney, Harvey Schmidt, Anthony Ferrante, and the magistrate. Ferrante is a fight manager well known in local (Philadelphia) sports circles."

Another reporter later told Jet magazine: "When top-ranking heavyweight contender Sonny Liston . . . stopped a twenty-nine-year-old woman motorist on a dark, deserted road in Philadelphia's Fairmount Park last June 12, he touched off a scandal which not only may have doomed his chances for a shot at the heavyweight crown, (but) the 'prank' may also damage the career of one of Philadelphia's most prominent Negro leaders.

"The Negro leader who has been caught up in the backwash of the swirling controversy is Harvey N. Schmidt, an attorney, who less than a fortnight ago was sworn in as the only (Negro) member of Philadelphia's Voter Registration Commission . . .

"On the same day that Schmidt was sworn into his new post, he announced he intends to file a legal action seeking damages against nationally syndicated sports columnist Dan Parker for an item written by Parker which Schmidt claims was both libelous and extremely damaging to his honesty and integrity.

"Parker had bluntly stated in his column that Mrs. Dolores Ellis, the young woman whom Liston had allegedly molested in Fairmount Park, had agreed to drop charges against the prizefighter after her attorney had accepted a twenty-five hundred dollar pay-off. "Schmidt, who was Mrs. Ellis' only attorney in the case, emphatically denied the pay-off charges. He said that Mrs. Ellis had agreed to drop her charges against Liston after the prizefighter made a public apology to her. Schmidt further insisted that his client had not been harmed by the prizefighter or his companion, Isaac Cooper, when they flashed a spotlight on her car in the manner of police and ordered her to halt.

" 'It is true they caused Mrs. Ellis a great deal of inconvenience and fear,' Schmidt said, 'but I could not say that these men did anything criminally wrong in respect to my client. That is the only reason which I agreed to allow my client to drop the matter.' "

In New York, Parker refused to divulge the source of his information but said he was certain of his facts and that they came from an irrefutable source.

On August 2, a hearing of the Liston re-arrest case was held and he was freed on five hundred dollars bail. Judge Victor Blanc, who said the case was blown up out of proportion, held Liston on a charge of turning off his automobile lights in order to avoid identification following the incident in Fairmount Park. Judge Blanc dismissed the charge of resisting arrest. The "dousing lights" case was turned over to a Grand Jury.

When Liston appeared before Commissioner of Jury Trials Joseph Scanlon early in September, he pleaded not guilty and through his attorney, Morton Witkin, and his manager, George Katz, asked for a jury trial. Scanlon set September 28 as the trial date.

Liston was acquitted.

During the trial, Judge Joseph Gold said that if Liston hadn't been involved, the case "would have been disposed of in the Magistrate's Court." Liston, perspiring profusely throughout the day, denied that he had fled the scene after turning out his lights. He said he had accidentally bumped the light switch while releasing the parking break. Marvin Halbert, an assistant district attorney, argued strenuously for conviction, declaring that "not a word of truth sprung from Liston's lips." But Judge Gold rejected Halbert's plea and commented:

"I think Mr. Liston is a very foolish man who has juvenile tendencies that will be knocked out of him one of these days."

When Liston was acquitted this time, he wiped perspiration from his ample brow in obvious relief and beamed:

"It's great! It's great!"

Witkin and Katz said their next move was to arrange the lifting of Liston's suspension so that he could resume his boxing career.

"He'll never make another mistake," Katz promised. "Now, we'll show the world he's a real, worthwhile champion. Patterson is going to fight us."

Where, or when, Katz wouldn't, or couldn't, say.

Meanwhile, Sonny was already working on his own rehabilitation, learning to read and write, reports were under the supervision of a Denver Catholic priest, Father Edward Murphy.

"It's a pleasure to have a neighbor like that. You can't imagine things like we heard and read happening to him when we saw an entirely different Sonny Liston."
—Miss Georgianna Myer, a Philadelphia resident.

CHAPTER XII

Shortly after Sonny Liston won the world's heavyweight championship, he announced that he was leaving Philadelphia. He spent most, if not all, of his house hunting time during the next two months in Chicago, where he and his wife Geraldine, sought a place with ten acres of land. He had not yet moved out of Philadelphia, however, when the author, aided by a reputable Philadelphia newsman, Malcolm Poindexter, sought an appraisal of the man, Sonny Liston, from people who most recently had had an ample opportunity either to know him or to observe him. Among these people were neighbors, associates in boxing, an attorney, an official of the State Athletic Commission.

"Few of us got to know him personally," said Miss Georgianna Myer, a neighbor who saw Liston as a friendly man with a smile, "but we all got used to seeing him come up and wave a cheery hello to us. The smile always followed and we'd smile and wave back. "It's a pleasure to have a neighbor like that. You can't imagine things like we heard and read happening to him when we saw an entirely different Sonny Liston. "He was so inconspicuous and quiet that we wondered if the guy ever talked. He tried to make friends and the people who were closest to him did become friendly. But he always really seemed most interested in the family."

Mrs. Gloria Wilkins, who lived two doors from Liston, also described him as a nice neighbor, "friendly and with a big smile." She said:

"We never had a minute's trouble with him in any way. We, too, found it hard to believe that he was the man pictured in the stories we read and on the radio and television. If he was, he certainly had us fooled. We'll miss him if he moves and we hope that maybe he and Mrs. Liston will change their minds. If they don't, then maybe they'll come back some day. We certainly hope so."

Attorney Morton Witkin said:

"I found him to be a man of integrity, honesty, and fair-dealing. As to what people are calling harassment by the Philadelphia police department, I have nothing to comment on that."

Liston had just recently been stopped—though no formal complaint was issued—for "driving too slow . . ."

"I think," Witkin continued, "that Sonny is a very human sort of person. He has an earthy sort of humor—mother wit, you might say—and like all people who have that make-up, he's quiet spoken and doesn't talk much. He takes his good, old time about answering. "I think Sonny is living down his past and his wife is a fine influence on him. She's tried in many ways to help him and it shows. Sonny appreciates it and talks about it.

"Another thing, Sonny is the hometown-type guy who never forgets his beginning. He's not too proud to go to the store and buy groceries. He's not too proud to go to the corner to buy his own newspaper. And he's not too proud to wipe off his own car, if it needs it.

"Say the guy has a good heart, that he's comical. And you won't be wrong a little bit.

"I'll never forget the comment he made months ago when a reporter asked him if he ever expected to fight for the title. Sonny's reply was, 'No—I always figured that was too steep a hill for me to climb.'"

Skinny Davidson is a former fighter and a well-respected trainer. He handles Harold Johnson, the light heavyweight champion. A man who believes Liston has "paid his debt to society," Davidson asked:

"How much more can they do to him? He's served time for whatever he did wrong years ago. He's been punished enough for whatever he did wrong since then.

"Let me show you a side of Sonny few people see. Take a guy like Georgie Gibbs"—a one-time fighter and trainer who is now blind— "I've seen Sonny come in after a big fight and walk over to Georgie and give him ten, fifteen and twenty-five dollars at a crack. He never asks for it back, and Gibbs isn't the only guy he's done it for. Anybody who's handicapped that Sonny sees, he goes right to helping them.

"As for what's happened to him in Philly, I think he's being harassed. Somebody wants to see somebody else in his spot. The guy's really got a big heart, but if they keep on talking about him and writing about him like they do in the hometown papers, then he's got to get a complex of some kind and that's what happened.

"Look, there's a lotta talk that Sonny's hooked up with the mob— even the Mafia. If he is, there's nothing he can do about it. *That's boxing.* He just got hooked in with the wrong crowd. But what can he do now? He's trying to live around it, but people don't seem to want to let him.

"You want my personal opinion? The law has made Liston what he is by harassing him. And, that's that."

John (Jack) Saunders is the secretary of the Pennsylvania State Athletic Commission.

"The Sonny Liston that people don't know," he said, "is a humorous-type guy who can keep you laughing with everything he says.

"I remember the time a writer asked him if he thought he could beat Patterson for the title. Sonny turned to the writer and asked him, 'Don't you think I can?'

"It's humor like that that's given the guy a reputation of having good, old mother wit. He's not real smart; he's not educated and he's not real intelligent. But he can hold a press conference and answer questions properly. He knows how to parry the wrong ones and he knows how to meet the ones that can do him some good.

"At the Kefauver hearing into mob activity in boxing, I remember Sonny was asked, "How many brothers and sisters have you?"

" 'Twenty-five, Sonny replied.

" 'Your dad was a champion in his own right,' Kefauver commented.

" 'He must have been, Sonny chortled wryly, 'he must have been.' "

Sonny has been close to Saunders ever since they met in Pittsburgh in 1956, when Sonny went there to fight Marty Marshall. After the fight, Saunders introduced himself to Sonny and the two struck up a lively conversation. It was Sonny confessing that he wanted to become a champion someday, and Saunders telling him that he had all the punch it would take.

Saunders was made aware of Sonny Liston's problems with the Philadelphia police. The fighter once complained to Jack that he felt he was being picked on. Later, he told Saunders that because it seemed to be an endless thing, he was thinking strongly of leaving Philadelphia to live in Chicago or Detroit.

"I recall he told me several times that he was hurt by the articles that were appearing in the papers," Saunders said. "He said he was going to leave the city and asked me what I thought of the idea.

" 'Sonny, do you feel like you're a bum, a hoodlum?' I asked him.

" 'No,' was the reply. 'I think I've paid for whatever I did wrong. I just want people to forget and let me forget, but they don't seem to want to let me.'

"I remember he told me he was trying to rehabilitate himself, and I asked him where he got that word from.

"Sonny told me that whenever he heard a word used that he didn't know, he would ask somebody what it meant and then he would use

114

it when the time came. Once he learned a word like that he would never forget it after that.

"That's the type of guy he is. He has faults just like any of us. He's trying to do right, if people will just let him. But they don't seem to want to.

"Sonny's no hardened criminal. I've seen the guy break down and cry in my office. He felt the treatment he was getting was totally unjustified. It hurt him—just like it would a little child—and he reacted the only way he knew how. If people could see him like that, they'd understand that he isn't the type guy he's pictured. No, the real Sonny Liston is a quiet, sensible guy with mother wit and humor to make a lot of people happy. All he wants is that they'll give him the same in return."

Willie Reddish, Liston's trainer, followed much the same line.

"Few people know Sonny—really know him," Reddish said. "He's never, for instance, passed a beggar, white or colored, on the street without giving him something. He didn't do it for effect. He never knew I even noticed, but I did. I'd watch out of the corner of my eye.

"I've also noticed how Sonny takes care of his wife and his mother. Any man who cares for his wife and mother like he does has his heart in the right place. Sonny's not only a regular fellow, but he's thoughtful as well. Whenever he visits some new city, he always thinks to buy something for the two 'women' in his life.

"As for his future as a fighter, the only thing I can say is that he'll lose his title to old age—but not to another heavyweight. The guy's built like an ox; he hits like a mule. I know. I've been a fighter and I've never seen a guy with that much power packed into his body. He hits like dynamite. I've watched him run guys right outta the ring . . ."

Ernest Terrell is a young heavyweight boxer.

This is what he had to say about Sonny Liston:

"I met Sonny in 1958 or 1959. I sparred with him for the Al Westphal fight and boxed with him for six weeks after that. You get to know a guy pretty good after that much experience.

"What I admire about Sonny is that he has a fighter's attitude. That separates him from the boys—separates him from every other fighter I know. He's in the ring to "kill you"—boxing parlance, not murder—"not to just beat you or knock you out—but to kill you. That's what it takes to be a good fighter and a convincing one. You gotta take that instinct into the ring with you. Otherwise, the other guy—the one you're fighting senses you're afraid or cautious and he takes quick advantage of you.

"Well, with Sonny, there's no such. He goes outta the corner and tries from the bell to blast your brains out. He's got power and determination. I know the guys he fights must feel it. You can even when you're sparring with him.

"Another thing, Sonny talks on his own level. He's a regular guy—not the kind now that he's on top to ignore the fellows he came along with . . . but the type to speak to you no matter where he sees you or happens to meet up with you.

"I remember we hadn't seen each other for months . . . and Sonny happened to walk into the gym one day and I was working out. He came way across the room to shake my hand and give me a big, broad hello. That's Sonny as I know him. What others think, I have nothing to do with. But, as for me—and a lotta guys who've been around us both—he's okay with a capital 'O.' "

On another occasion, another Philadelphian, George Katz, had this pertinent statement to make about Liston:

"Sonny has a complex about being with people. He thinks he only belongs with guys like himself. He never knew his position . . . how important he was. That's his main trouble."

"You now stand at the final crossroads of your career. You have been at crossroads before; this is the last one. What you do after today will determine the course of the rest of your life and your career."
—Alfred Klein, Pennsylvania State Athletic commissioner, speaking to Sonny Liston at the time Sonny was suspended from boxing.

CHAPTER XIII

During the time Sonny Liston was in Denver, Colorado, for his fight with Zora Folley—July 18, 1960—he met and became friendly with a Catholic priest, Father Edward P. Murphy of the St. Ignatius Loyola Church. After Sonny was suspended by the Pennsylvania State Athletic Commission, he went to Denver, placing himself under the direction of Father Murphy in an educational rehabilitation program.

The event was widely publicized.

Liston's apparent willingness to seek help struck a responsive chord in the hearts of many people, including his friends, who wanted to see him not only fight for the world's heavyweight championship but also make a better man, and citizen, out of himself.

The cynics, though, saw nothing more than a "build-up" in the association of Sonny Liston and Father Murphy.

One cynic inferred in print that this was a part of the build-up which would clean up Liston sufficiently to enable him to fight Patterson and Father Murphy was coldly referred to in this article as a "house priest."

There was, along about this time, an astonishing report that Liston himself wanted to become a Catholic priest—Sonny cleaned that one up with a simple reminder: He was married!

But Sonny, a confessed Methodist, according to his mother, expressed great interest in the Catholic religion and in the prospect of *joining* the church.

Assisting Father Murphy in the educational rehabilitation of Liston was the Reverend William Wade, a member of the St. Louis University faculty. Reverend Wade was spending the summer in Denver.

As planned, Sonny was to live three or four weeks with Father Murphy in the church rectory. Then Mrs. Liston was to join the fighter and they were to live in a home nearby.

Father Murphy and Reverend Wade concentrated on four areas of education and rehabilitation in their work with Liston: reading and writing, humility and understanding.

Liston also found time to do roadwork and otherwise keep himself in shape for fighting.

In a statement made shortly after his arrival in Denver, Liston admitted that the publicity about his suspension from boxing hadn't done him any good "but it wasn't as bad as the newspapers say it was. People are easily led against you and it's harder to get them to go along with you."

He also said that this publicity about his suspension and other troubles stemmed from "newspapermen doing anything to make a story. It's like a fight—I do everything to win."

Liston expressed the hope that he would be reinstated soon and would be permitted to engage Patterson in a title bout. "Patterson says it's the mob that keeps him from fighting me, but I'm the only mob he's worried about."

Father Murphy encouraged Liston to believe that he would, indeed, be reinstated in boxing.

"If Sonny does a good job," Father Murphy said, "the suspension eventually will be lifted. They can't take away a man's livelihood."

Sometime later, Father Murphy said:

"I see a lot of good in Sonny. What he needs more than anything else is good direction. I try to give it to him. When boxing is on his mind, he's a dedicated man."

In *Ebony* magazine, writer Allan Morrison viewed the Sonny Liston-Father Murphy relationship in a psychological light.

"For the second time in his life," Morrison said, "he had found in Father Murphy the Freudian father figure his childhood lacked. The first had been Father Alois Stevens in Missouri. Both were gentle, understanding men who convinced him that he had a sound future. "The presence of a fatherly symbol is important to Liston's well-being. His attorney and main adviser, Morton Witkin, a courtly shrewd and amiable man, currently comes closer to filling the role. . . . Like his two Jesuit predecessors, Witkin is white and totally unlike Sonny's father in manner and attitude. He treats Liston with the respect he needs so desperately and never tries to impose his own views on him. "Sonny has a mind of his own," is Witkin's belief."

Morrison also ferreted out some of Liston's thoughts along racial lines, one being his contention that "in this world, if you're colored, anything you do has to be twice as good as the white man. Most colored boys who go into boxing are poor and boxing offers them a chance to make money, to get somewhere."

Liston also revealed why he disliked Patterson. "I have a little dislike for Patterson, but it's not because he wouldn't agree to fight me for so long but because he hasn't fought any colored boys since becoming champion. Patterson draws the color line against his own race. We have a hard enough time as it is in this white man's world." Actually, though this charge had been made against Patterson by others, in the *Negro Press* even, it was unfair, at least to this extent: Patterson had defended the title against one Negro, Tommy (Hurricane) Jackson, whom he knocked out in the tenth round at New York on July 29, 1957. All others of Patterson's title defenses up to his meeting with Liston, however, were made against white opponents, most of them regarded by many to be unworthy challengers, particularly so since such capable fighters as Liston himself, Zora Folley, Cleveland Williams and, perhaps, Eddie

Machen—all of these Negroes—were around, willing and eager to meet the champion.

Four months after he'd begun his educational rehabilitation program with Father Murphy, Liston revealed that "I feel like a new person . . . We meet and talk every day and I feel I have found a true friend for the first time. I am also taking instructions and will join the Catholic Church.

"I am learning for the first time how to live, how people should treat each other. I had it tough when I was a kid. I got into a lot of trouble because I hardly knew right from wrong."

When Father Murphy was asked sometime later if he thought Liston who, by that time, had been reinstated in boxing, had *rehabilitated* himself, he said, "I don't like that word. *Reorientation* is better. When Sonny came here, we sat down and had many talks. He lived next door with our housekeeper for months. He confided in me. I visited his training camp two weeks ago. He's doing just wonderful."

Father Murphy was told that police in St. Louis doubted reports of Liston's rehabilitation or reorientation.

"Down there," Father Murphy responded, "I guess he was a tough guy. He wants to be champion. Joe Louis is Sonny's idol. He wants to be like Joe. He doesn't smoke or drink. Out here, he was on his own. He won the respect of everyone. A lot of policemen are his friends. He is fond of children and the kids are crazy about him. I want to get him into the fight against juvenile delinquency. He did a good job when he spoke to the boys at the home. He told them they can't make it if they don't behave themselves. They listened to him." Sonny wasn't especially loquacious when a New York writer persisted in questioning him about what he'd done and learned at Denver.

"I've been learning to be around different kinds of people," Sonny said.

"*What kind?*"

"The right kind," Sonny said.

He was pressed for a more expansive explanation.

"There are only two kinds of people. Good and bad, right?"

Sonny let out a little more of his disapproval of newspaper reporting methods.

"The newspapers," he said, "always put me down as a bad guy. You can't live it down. They always bring it up. When I got in the last trouble, they had big headlines. When I was cleared, they had this much"—showing a small space between his thumb and forefinger—"whatever there was is over but will people believe it? Will they believe me?"

"In the fight before that with Howard King, Sonny got only about $600. Barone had him then. Tom Bolan, the promoter, told me not to worry. He gave me a message from Patterson. He said Patterson had given him his word to fight Liston in 1962. I believed Tom . . . But I asked him if Patterson would put it in writing. He said, no, but told me Patterson's word was as good as his bond."
—George Katz, former manager of Sonny Liston.

CHAPTER XIV

Jack Johnson chased Tommy Burns over hill and dale and sea, all the way from the United States of America to Australia, before he was finally able to step into the ring as the challenger for the world's heavyweight championship, which he won easily at Sydney, Australia, on December 26, 1908. Johnson was, according to many experts, the greatest heavyweight fighter who ever lived.

Years later, Harry Wills took up a chase after Jack Dempsey. He never got the fight he wanted.

Liston's chase after Patterson certainly must be recorded as the most *troublesome* effort to get another man into the ring; it was the most tedious, next to Johnson's, probably the most controversial; and, on a general appraisal, the most drawn-out episode involving the worthiest challenger and a champion in ages.

Liston's difficulties with the law, his record, his questionable associates were, of course, legitimate blocks in his pathway, although it must be said that segments of boxing which had never been renowned for previous righteousness suddenly assumed a startling holiness when Liston's name was mentioned. Patterson was managed by a man—some called him Cautious Cus D'Amato— who had never shown any great desire to see Patterson step into the ring with a tough opponent and Liston's problems were a handy excuse. There is no reason to suggest that either Patterson or D'Amato was obligated to contribute to Liston's personal welfare; yet it seems logical to conclude that if Liston had been granted a more direct pathway to the title bout, his difficulties in Philadelphia might never have arisen. He would have been training for his big moment. What about the legitimate beef against Liston's associates, the suspected mob-connected people said to have been pulling his strings? *What about, then, the strange shenanigans leading up to D'Amato's own suspension in New York?*

There are several interesting stages of the chase, which may be roughly established as:

1) The stage of getting the Man to say, yes;

2) The New York stage; and,

3) The Chicago stage.

The overall chase encompasses the ludicrous fight Liston had with a man whom he jokingly calls "Quickfall," and a sub-stage involving virtually every city which houses a boxing ring. All these towns were brought into the picture, at least publicity-wise, after New York said, nay, and before Chicago nodded affirmatively.

The thought occurs that not nearly so much would have been written about the projected Liston-Patterson match if boxing, overall, had been more alive in the heavyweight division during this period of time; if Patterson, especially, had been striving to emulate Joe Louis, or even Ezzard Charles, insofar as keeping a jump on the title was concerned. Patterson's penchant for sitting on it, or merely dangling it before safe non-entities, certainly left a news void in the division, a void which speculation about Liston, period, and about Liston-Patterson, on the other hand, partially filled.

Liston brought some of this up during the Senate investigation after Senator Everett Dirksen of Illinois asked him if boxing was slipping as a sport.

"The onliest thing that can bring it back to life is a guy who fights, like Joe Louis," Liston said. "Everybody and anybody, not like

Patterson, who plays around. He picks Ingemar Johansson, Brian London, and Pete Rademacher. People don't want to see them. If him and me fought, we would draw a bigger gate than him and Johansson."

"Then you have no sermon," Dirksen said, "no suggestions."

"Don't sit on the title, that's all," Liston said.

"You have no suggestions," said Dirksen. "I'd say you're short on words, long on clout."

"That's the way I try to be," said Liston.

After Liston returned home to Philadelphia following his April 25, 1960, first-round knockout of Roy Harris at Houston, Texas, he learned that the National Boxing Association had named him the No. 1 contender for the world's heavyweight title, an action which catapulted Sonny ahead of Patterson, who had lost the crown to Ingemar Johansson via a surprising third-round knockout at New York City on June 26, 1959—and was now spending a year brooding about it and building up steam for his (Patterson's) rematch with Johansson June 20, 1960. [Patterson, of course, regained the title from Johansson on the latter date, becoming the first heavyweight to lose and regain the championship.]

The news of his ascension to the No. 1 challenger's position brought no public smile to Sonny's face.

"I could be No. 1 for a long time," he observed, rather sadly. "If the National Boxing Association would make the champion fight me— then I'd have a reason to smile."

Liston said it would just be his luck to have Patterson regain the title and stretch out his period of delay another year or two. And if Johansson wins?

"That Archie Moore is pretty cute," Sonny said. "He could get in ahead of me. He's already trying."

This bit of dialogue shows that Liston had only the shallowest of hopes that his title chance was soon forthcoming. He belabored a point of logic: "Anybody who wants a title match ought to be forced to get by me first." He thought the National Boxing Association should make such a ruling. "But I'd have to see a thing like that to believe it."

Liston suggested that he'd like to meet both Patterson and Johansson on the same night, in the same ring, simultaneously.

But suppose one of them got behind him?

"That's what the ropes and corners are for," said Liston—and who wants to call this man dumb? "They couldn't get behind me there."

Many knowledgeable boxing observers declare that the return-bout clause in boxing title contracts is a curse to the sport. It is a means of prolonging the competitive status of losers and it, therefore, depreciates the chances of worthy challengers. After Liston demolished Patterson, he was still tied to a return-bout clause which enabled Patterson to claim an even split in the money (though thoroughly discredited as a fighter) and to select the site of the match. After Patterson regained the title from Johansson on June 20, 1960, he did not go on to fight Liston. No. He fought Johansson again, at Miami Beach on March 13, 1961, winning by a sixth-round knockout.

Liston was on hand to see the match—and he was left singularly unimpressed by Patterson's fighting ability. Liston, it should be noted, never wavered in his beliefs and opinions and statements about Patterson, which is more than can be said for many who were numbered among his—Sonny's—chief critics.

If Patterson would meet me in a title fight, said Liston, "I'd give him all the money!"

All sorts of conversation was manufactured after the Patterson-Johansson bout in Miami Beach.

"I'd take on the champ tomorrow if he would (fight me)," said Liston, who'd knocked out Howard King in three rounds in the same town less than a week earlier.

"I don't know how Patterson can take it," Liston responded to a question. "I don't know how hard Johansson can take it. I won't get the chance because of Cus D'Amato." Liston was to walk into D'Amato's office one day, startling that man, and ask him point blank why he wouldn't permit Patterson to fight him. He received an answer something like, "You know what you have to do," a reference to his publicized demands that Liston cleanse himself, in one way or another.

But Liston was assured the backing of the National Boxing Association. Following a meeting of the National Boxing Association's executive committee, a statement was issued. "We have decided to support Liston as the rightful challenger. He shouldn't be condemned because of the testimony before the executive committee."

Meanwhile, various people were attempting to purchase Liston's managerial contract from Pep Barone. Barone, however, was still talking like a fighter's manager.

"I'll guarantee Patterson a $1 million to fight Liston," he said in Miami Beach. "It won't be necessary to raise the money. He can have all of the television rights and the gate. Bill Fugazy and Roy Cohn (fight promoters) have been talking to us, but they have angles. Meade Johnson has a $4 million company and has asked to have first shot, if I sell the contract."

Julius November, Patterson's lawyer, had a few words to say about Liston:

"He's slow but he has a heavy punch. *Liston may be our next big money fight.*"

This was one of the earliest, if not the first, positive statement regarding Liston ever made by a member of the Patterson camp. Of course, it should be noted, November didn't say how many "little-money" fights might be okayed by Patterson, D'Amato and Company before Liston was approved.

Later in March, 1961, Liston—still under command from heavyweight King Patterson to clean up his managerial connections—was "offered" a fight with Johansson in Sweden on September 14. Edwin Ahlqvist, Johansson's fistic adviser, offered Liston a $125,000 guarantee for the match. There was hypocrisy here. When Johansson was champion, he, too, had black-listed Liston because of his managerial set-up. Now, though, when Johansson was "down," fighting Liston was okay, fine, approved, nice, clean!

"We'd be delighted to take such a match," Barone said at first. "In fact, we'd like to fight Johansson and Patterson the same night."

But, later, he cautiously said, "You don't go into a thing like this before finding out how solid the offer is. I still need to be convinced Ahlqvist means business."

Ahlqvist said the Liston-Johansson bout could be held in a stadium seating sixty-three thousand fans and said he could count on a gate ranging between six and eight hundred thousand dollars. He said he was willing, prepared, to deposit a minimum guarantee of one hundred and twenty-five thousand dollars in an American bank for Liston four days before the fight. Ahlqvist's idea was that the winner of the Liston-Johansson bout would meet Patterson in June, 1962. Ahlqvist had also suggested that Patterson should fight Henry Cooper, the British Empire heavyweight champion in his next bout. All of which boiled down to this: Ahlqvist was doing a helluva lot of match-making in his mind.

Barone said he'd have to meet Ahlqvist personally to discuss the matter further.

But, for Liston, there soon came more bad news.

California banned him!

Dr. Dan O. Kilroy, chairman of the California Athletic Commission, said on April Fool's Day, 1961, that Liston would never be allowed to fight there under his current management.

"From what we have learned," Kilroy said, "Joseph Barone, who is Liston's manager of record, is no manager at all. Liston is managed by underworld figures who are hidden. I have not polled the other four members of the Commission on this matter, but I am as sure as I am of my own name that they feel as I do." Kilroy said that the only way Liston could fight in California was to prove definitely that "he has rid himself of his underworld ties. And I just don't see how Liston could do that without a machine gun."

Hot words soon poured out of Allentown, Pennsylvania, where Pep Barone lived, but they weren't directed to Kilroy. Barone was hot under the collar, or above the collar, about Patterson's excuse for not fighting Liston, and this heat led into an interesting monologue.

"Patterson must be reading comic books," said Barone, for an opener. Patterson had set off the verbal torrent by charging again that Liston was controlled by the mob.

"Patterson says he wants to fight in New York," Barone continued. "He says he's worried about me. What about his manager, Cus D'Amato? Why hasn't he a license in New York? He must have done something wrong . . .

"Why does Patterson have to fight in New York? All that is needed is a promoter and Tele-Prompter. I'll find a promoter and then I'll bring my lawyer and sit down with Patterson. I'm new to closed-circuit television and I'll need my lawyer for protection. Patterson knows about Tele-Prompter . .

"I think Patterson should clean up his own connections. Then let him fight Liston, as he should. I'm for having a nice clean fight."

But Barone's days were numbered.

Patterson's campaign was taking its toll.

In April, 1961, Liston announced that "I'm asking Pep to give up his contract with me so I can get a title fight." Their five-year contract reportedly had two years to go. "The way it is now, Patterson won't fight me because of the men he says are behind Pep." Liston said that if Barone refused, he'd quit fighting. He said that before he'd sign with a new manager, "I'll ask Senator Kefauver to investigate him and make sure he's okay."

It was rumored around that Joe Louis, who had visited Liston a month earlier, was instrumental in Sonny's decision to rid himself of Barone.

Bigger news came on April 19.

The news? Liston had purchased his contract from Pep Barone for seventy-five thousand dollars, which would be paid out of Sonny's earnings over the next two years.

"I don't see how Patterson will be able to walk down the street now, unless he gives me a fight," Liston said.

But, in New York, despite wire photos showing Liston posed with a notary public, Joanne Koch, who was affixing a seal to the agreement whereby Liston purportedly purchased Barone's contract, Cus D'Amato said he was unimpressed by the news.

"Whatever plans Patterson may have, already have been made," D'Amato said. "He (Liston) is not included in these plans. He should have done this a long time ago. Anyone who may try to impose Liston upon Patterson, I will take to court. We will find out once and for all that nobody can make anybody fight anybody else."

Yet there appeared to be confusion, or disagreement, or something of the kind, in the Patterson ranks, too. Al Bolan, an official of Championship Sports, Inc., a new promotional corporation, said that his brother, Tom, the corporation president, had been in touch with Patterson. Al said "Patterson told Tom that he has said all along he was anxious to fight Liston but that he was on record that it would be up to Liston to clean house and when he has done this convincingly, he can talk about fighting him. Patterson indicated that inasmuch as Liston had mentioned satisfying the Kefauver Committee, which brought this matter to a head, that that would seem to be Liston's first step."

Barone again denied that he had any link with Carbo or Palermo and said Patterson was using them as an excuse because he was afraid of Liston.

Patterson himself said, referring to the latest news, that Liston "will have to show me that he is free of all harmful outside influences. When he does that, he will be entitled to his chance."

Barone said he had been offered a hundred and fifty thousand dollars for Liston's contract but was taking less (half!) "because I don't want to deprive him of a heavyweight title fight."

Supposition was that Liston's new manager—he refused to divulge a name—would merely take orders from Sonny who, like Patterson seemed to be by this time, would be his own boss.

Senator Kefauver expressed qualified delight on hearing the news of the Barone-Liston deal.

"If this is a valid sale," he said, "it will be a big boost to clean professional boxing."

The purchase agreement between Liston and Barone was signed in the Allentown law offices of Eugene J. Gorman, brother-in-law of Federal Judge J. Cullen Ganey.

There was a report that Joe Louis would become Liston's manager, but Sonny denied this, saying he had several men in mind and would make his decision within a week or two.

"Is my house clean enough now for him (Patterson) to give me a fight," Liston wanted to know, "or was he only looking for an excuse to duck me when he told the world he wouldn't fight me until I cleaned house?"

Meanwhile, investigative-minded senators in Washington "stared hard" at the seventy-five-thousand-dollar Liston-Barone deal and there were suggestions that an inquiry should be held because this financial figure was "such a bargain."

Rocky Marciano, former heavyweight champion, got into the act next.

He said Russ Murray, a dog-track owner, had offered Liston a hundred and fifty thousand dollars for Sonny's managerial contract.

"Russ Murray is making a sealed bid for Liston's contract," Marciano said. "If the sale goes through, Russ wants me to be Liston's manager."

Marciano said he would like to manage a heavyweight champion and "Liston obviously has the potential. I think a combination of Russ Murray and myself would satisfy everybody. Liston's new background must satisfy Patterson. And Liston himself has said that his new owners or manager must satisfy Senator Estes Kefauver, chairman of the sub-committee investigating sports." Among others seeking to get in on the Liston deal was Frank De Rice, a seventy-one-year-old resident of Montreal.

In ex-fighter Lew Tendler's Philadelphia restaurant on May 10, 1961, Sonny Liston disclosed the name of his new manager, George Katz, manager of ex-fighter Gil Turner. At the same time, the Pennsylvania State Athletic Commission announced that Liston had been granted a boxing license in that state for the first time and that the Commission had approved the contractual arrangements with Katz.

Katz who, of course, we know was to foul out too, lost no time in making his voice heard. Dwarfed in size by the giant Liston, he made up for it in verbal clout.

"Now, let's get one thing straight," he said. "George Katz is not Sonny Liston's agent and not an employee. George Katz is Sonny Liston's manager."

Disclosure that under their two-and-a-half-year agreement he would receive only 10 percent of Liston's earnings after expenses, contrasted to the usual managerial cut of $33^{1}/_{3}$ percent, did not take any wind out of Katz's sails.

"Ten percent of about $10 million isn't bad," he said. "Besides, the circumstances are not ordinary. I'm taking over a fighter who's already the No. 1 contender."

Katz announced that "we want to fight Patterson as soon as possible but we're not barring any opponent. Yes, we'd be interested in a match with Ingemar Johansson."

The State Athletic Commission had several items to announce, among them:

It had scrutinized Katz's record and found it to be above reproach.

It had recommended that the National Boxing Association ratify its actions.

It would handle all the money involved in the Liston Barone deal and place the money "directly in Barone's hands."

"When I was in Washington," said Commissioner Alfred M. Klein, "Senator Kefauver asked me to see that Liston's managerial problems were straightened out and now that has been accomplished."

It was said that Katz was a tender, gentle, paternalistic kind of fight manager!

The next important news front was Geneva, where Ingemar Johansson claimed it would be fun to beat Sonny Liston and added,

"I don't think he is unbeatable; I think I can lick him." Johansson proposed to fight Liston before the year (1961) was out, and Katz said Liston had a guarantee of two hundred thousand dollars plus ten thousand dollars for expenses, for the fight.

Of course, Liston's difficulties with the law in Philadelphia during the spring and summer of 1961 knocked a little dent in all these plans and proposals.

On June 26, the *Associated Negro Press* asked a question:

"Is the National Boxing Association gunning for Sonny Liston?"

Then the *Associated Negro Press* revealed that the National Boxing Association was conducting a poll to determine whether or not Liston should be dropped from its ratings. *Associated Negro Press* described the poll as being "hush-hush, confidential." If it was hush hush, confidential, then the leak had sprung in St. Louis where Bob Hunter, then sports editor of the *St. Louis Argus*, had learned that a "very confidential" letter had been sent to Missouri State Athletic Commissioner Charles W. Pian.

According to Hunter, Pian reacted negatively to the National Boxing Association's letter, responding thusly:

"In regard to your poll that you are taking on Sonny Liston, I myself do not wish to vote against him. I think he should be kept on the list as the No. 1 contender for the heavyweight championship. If he is proven guilty [of the Philadelphia charges, already detailed here], then that is another story . . .

"I will wait and see what the court has to say on the subject, for they are in a better position than I to know if he is guilty or not."

The *Associated Negro Press* noted that "if Liston is ousted from the National Boxing Association ratings as a result of the poll, it will make it easier for champion Floyd Patterson and his querulous manager, Cus D'Amato, to ignore Liston's demands for a title match."

Meanwhile, Katz declared that "I will fight them (the National Boxing Association) with every cent I can beg or borrow" if "they" attempted to oust Liston from the ratings.

While Liston was having his difficulties in Philadelphia, Floyd Patterson was in Highland Mills, New York, training for a bout with tenth-ranked Tom McNeeley, whom few fight fans had ever heard of, but was thinking of Sonny, in a detached way.

His comment about Liston's troubles was this:

"Liston is a grown man. I don't want to say anything more about him."

When the prospect of an eventual Patterson-Liston bout was pressed, Floyd said: "If and when I fight him, Liston will be the big fight of my career. He's a good fighter; he's a dangerous fighter."

When Liston was suspended by the Pennsylvania State Athletic Commission, the action set off a chain reaction. Sonny was dropped from the National Boxing Association ratings and Henry Cooper of England was elevated to his No. 1 challenger position. The National Boxing Association, active in forty-seven states, declared that Liston would be re-rated if and when he is re-instated, a declaration that sounded much like a Cassius Clay poem. California was heard from. "Liston hasn't got a prayer of getting a license to box in our state," said Douglas Hayden of the Athletic Commission.

There was some talk of Liston meeting Ingemar Johansson in Canada, but Jim Crowley of the Pennsylvania State Athletic Commission, formerly one of Notre Dame's celebrated "Four Horsemen" of football, said: "They wouldn't be able to fight in Montreal or Toronto until the suspension is lifted."

Johansson, though, wasn't averse to taking the fight. He said, "I wouldn't take the fight if I didn't know I could beat him."

While Johansson was talking, Liston was in Denver, working with Father Murphy on another project—his redemption!

On October 16, 1961, Patterson signed an official contract to meet Tom McNeeley in a title bout, fifteen rounds, in Toronto on December 4. There was speculation that a Sonny Liston-Albert Westphal bout would be held in Philadelphia the same night as a part of a fistic double-header on theatre television. Westphal, a German, wasn't officially rated and Liston was yet under suspension in Pennsylvania, but somebody knew what was happening.

134

What was happening was this:

The wheels were turning for Liston's reinstatement in Pennsylvania. He had, of course, been acquitted twice of the charges of impersonating an officer, dousing his lights, and so on.

When his reinstatement was announced, Alfred Klein explained:

"It has never been the purpose of the Commission to destroy the career of Liston or any other athlete. The unique circumstances of the program projected for December 4 present to Liston an opportunity which, if now denied to him, could well accomplish irreparable damage to him, both as a championship contender and as a man. The Commission is not prepared to be the instrument of such damage."

Red Smith, the noted sports writer, commented:

"Liston's score in Missouri was paid off years ago. There are no actions pending against him in Pennsylvania. The Reverend Edward Murphy, who has been teaching him reading, writing and rectitude in Denver since his last arrest, testifies to his recent good behavior. As to the vehicle for his return to prominence in the heavyweight division, about all that can be said is that Westphal's credentials as an opponent are on par with McNeeley's as a championship contender."

When Liston learned that he'd regained his National Boxing Association rating, he exclaimed:

"That's good, that's good. Now I won't have to knock off that Britisher to get to that title. Maybe I don't have to fight Cooper now to show who's who."

Sonny said he'd go to Denver to train for his fight with Westphal. And, meanwhile, a funny thing happened: In the new ratings, McNeeley, Patterson's next opponent, was knocked out of the first ten!

In the meantime, Liston appeared in Chicago, where he applied for a renewal of his 1959 license in Illinois, so that he could fight a four-round exhibition with Ernie Terrell on a card topped by Joey Giardello and Jesse Smith. Sonny was early in arrival and was present, along with Archie Moore, another gate hiker, at a publicity bash. On being asked why he'd come so early, Sonny said:

"I've been on the bad side of the ledger so much that I wanted to be on the good side for a change."

A few days later, Liston had something more to say about Floyd Patterson:

"Patterson is a soft touch. Other guys dropped him, and I'd like to. If I knocked him down as many times as Johansson did in Miami, and he kept getting up, I'd quit, and retire from fighting."

On December 4, 1961, one of boxing's weirdos occurred.

Sonny Liston fought Albert Westphal in Philadelphia as a part of a televised double-header, knocked him out in the first round and, without changing clothes, sought out a television set so he could sit and watch the drama starring Floyd Patterson and Tom McNeeley. Still dressed in a white robe—"no sense changing clothes; didn't even work up a sweat!"—Liston sat in the press room under the stands at Municipal Auditorium, sipped orange juice, and talked about both his recent "fight" and the "fight" on television.

Westphal was a five-foot, seven-and-one-half-inch, German baker who succumbed to Sonny's assault at one minute and fifty-eight seconds of the first round and then, on recovery, displayed a brand of precise honesty seldom seen in boxing. On being asked if he'd like a return match with Sonny, Westphal forthrightly said, "No!"

Liston was asked what punches he'd used to kayo Westphal in a full two minutes.

"Left jab, right hand," Sonny said.

"How did it feel looking down there at Westphal?"

"It felt good."

No smiling.

While Patterson was waiting for the bell to sound off the beginning of his bout in Toronto, Sonny said of Floyd:

"If he was here, I'd go back and fight without even taking a shower. The only sweat I worked up was when I loosened up in the corner."

When McNeeley survived the first round with Patterson, Liston said: "They should be talking about it now." Patterson had knocked

McNeeley down three times at a point in the third round when someone asked Sonny what he thought of Floyd's performance so far.

"Maybe it's taking him a long time to figure him out," Sonny said. "Some people use adding machines and some people use their heads. Sooner or later he comes up with the right number."

Patterson floored McNeeley eleven times and won on a knockout at two minutes and fifty-one seconds of the fourth round. Former world's heavyweight champion Jersey Joe Walcott was the referee. After Patterson won, Liston suddenly cut off his flow of sarcastic remarks because "I don't want to blow my chance" for a title bout.

He said Patterson looked better beating McNeeley, an inept foe, obviously, than he did while whipping Johansson. "But," Sonny asked, "who am I to pass opinion on anyone? I do that in the ring."

It was following this twin bill that President Kennedy assertedly remarked that both fights were mismatches—that Patterson should have been fighting Liston and McNeeley should have been fighting Westphal.

In Toronto, Patterson had passed the ball to D'Amato when he was asked when and where he would defend the title against Liston.

"Liston knows what he must do to get a fight with Patterson," D'Amato said. "If he does it, he knows he can sign for the fight tomorrow."

D'Amato refused to explain what it was that Liston "must do."

By now, speculation was rife that Patterson and Liston would actually meet. Someone asked Liston if he thought his quick knockout of Westphal had frightened Patterson.

"How long have I been the No. 1 challenger?" Sonny asked.

"A year and a half."

"That's how long he's been scared of me."

Liston had always been publicized as being either illiterate or semi-illiterate, though a few more discerning observers like Fathers Stevens and Murphy, found a solid base of intelligence and/or mother wit in him. In the final analysis, it was Liston's continual harping on the

137

subject of Patterson's "fear" that forced the fight as much as anything else, including boxing justice.

The sensitive, proud Patterson could not ignore Liston's jibes. Calculated plan, or not, Sonny touched a nerve when he said Floyd was afraid. Once Liston was quoted as calling Patterson a coward and Patterson reportedly became so upset about it that he declared that he'd have to fight the No. 1 challenger, either in the ring or in the street.

The day after he knocked out McNeeley, Patterson said he would like to meet Liston next, if a few obstacles were removed to D'Amato's satisfaction.

"I would definitely give Liston a chance," Patterson said. "The date, place, and all that stuff will come later. According to my manager—*or should I say, adviser?*— there still are a few obstacles. *There are no obstacles to me.* But my *manager* says they are pretty serious ones."

"There are conditions to be removed," D'Amato elucidated. "If he really wants the fight, he can remove them. He is well aware of them. They are removable by anyone who wants a heavyweight title bout. There is nobody in the world I'd like to have Floyd fight and beat rather than Liston. That would establish Floyd in the minds of even the most Doubting Thomas."

The "removable objects" of which D'Amato spoke were, of course, the questionable associates still rumored to be pulling Liston's managerial reins. At this point it became fairly obvious, whenever D'Amato and Patterson could be drawn into conversation on the subject, that there was a division of opinion and a subtle suggestion that D'Amato was not as strong in the decision-making department of Floyd Patterson Enterprises as he had once been.

The subtle hint was to be found in Patterson's choice of words— manager or *adviser*. A bolder hint was obvious in his statement that "there are no obstacles to me." In other words, although Patterson had hidden behind the smoke-screen of Liston's allegedly improper associations, now, though it was widely presumed that nothing had been changed at the base of Sonny's managerial set-up, Patterson had come to the point of a decision to take on Liston, for better or for worse.

Patterson desperately craved recognition as a great champion. He knew he hadn't gained this recognition. He was aware that, no matter how he and D'Amato twisted and turned, Floyd could never be convincingly the "best man" as long as Liston dogged his tail. And, always, there was Sonny, standing in the wings, telling one and all within ear-shot, "He's afraid to fight me."

After Liston destroyed Westphal in the "comparative double-header," the pendulum of the press began to swing discernibly in his favor. He had, obviously, done everything he could in the ring to justify his right to a fight. There were no other challengers worthier than he; it would have been nothing less than blasphemy on the championship if Patterson continued to evade him. D'Amato's pleas for the cleansing of Liston had won some public sympathy, but the line was wearing thin.

Pete Hamill got down to the nitty-gritty of it when he said, "One of the hardiest myths of sports is the one that describes the heavyweight champion of the world as a heroic figure admired by the young."

"I have received hundreds of letters about Liston," said Nat Fleischer, editor of Ring magazine, "and the average person says, 'Yes, Liston should get a shot.' They say that so long as the fellow has been cleared by the courts, he should be given the opportunity that any man gets when he starts all over. If they don't want him to box, then they should bar him throughout the world, and not just in certain states. I feel approximately the same way, even though I hate to see him in there because the man's record has not done boxing any good."

Bob Burnes's thinking matched Fleischer's.

"He's certainly no angel," Burnes said, "and I'm the first one to admit that. But he served time in the penitentiary for the only serious crime he ever committed. He is easily misled by anyone who wants to lead him and he had the misfortune to run into people who liked to mislead him.

"I still feel, as far as my own personal part in it is concerned, that Father Stevens and I got him out of the penitentiary because we believed that one way an illiterate man had a chance to rehabilitate himself was with his fists.

"I feel that since getting out, his conduct has been far from circumspect. But it is no worse than many other people in boxing today and I believe that he's earned the right to contest for the heavyweight title."

Sports Illustrated conducted a poll of notable people, who were asked whether or not Liston should be given a shot at the heavyweight title. As *Sports Illustrated* explained, "One view is that in this day and age we cannot afford a United States heavyweight champion with Liston's unsavory record. A second is that he ought not to be allowed a fight until he can prove he is free of mob control. A third attitude is that Liston owes society nothing—he is not on probation or on parole or out on bail—and is entitled to a chance to make good. Finally, there are those who contend emphatically that they don't care what kind of man Liston may be outside the ring, as long as he is a good fighter inside it."

In response to *Sports Illustrated* poll, John G. Bonomi, Special Assistant Attorney General of New York State, said: "I question whether Liston, as of now, should even be licensed, let alone get a shot at the heavyweight title. I don't believe he has demonstrated any real rehabilitation. Also, he hasn't gotten rid of his underworld connections . . . However, I don't think Liston should be barred forever. While I personally don't expect him to change that much, I think it's possible that he could get rid of his gangster associates and improve his record enough to fight in the future."

Jackie Robinson, former baseball star, said: "Personally, I would like to see Floyd fight Liston, although I think Patterson would demolish the man. To prove himself to the public, I think Patterson has to fight him . . . However, I am disappointed that Liston's record isn't better and realize that Patterson has to think of more people than just himself."

Branch Rickey, baseball executive, said: "It's plain greed on the part of somebody that brings a character of that type into public view.

I tried to believe I had enough respect for Patterson that he wouldn't get down to that level. Boxing is sick—a messy business . . ."

Sir David Harrington Angus Douglas, the twelfth Marquis of Queensberry, said: "I would have rather thought it wasn't all that relevant whether or not Liston was a good character. If he's not in prison at the moment, he must currently be legally straight. If he's a very good boxer, he must be entitled to a fight with Patterson. You might as well say I won't fight somebody because he's not Christian or not white . . . Your efficiency as a boxer, swimmer or runner is not terribly related to how nice a chap you are . . ."

Author Harry Golden said: "Does each state have its set of rules? Why, then, should there be a problem if this Sonny Liston qualifies as a candidate? I once sat in a pool hall and watched the great Babe Ruth shoot a game. Such language! I knew Ty Cobb and some of the things he did. Great athletes. Marvelous. But I would not want any son of mine growing up like Ruth or Cobb . . ."

For the doubters and worriers, Liston offered, through Morton Witkin, a unique plan.

"He's ready, willing and anxious to fight Patterson anywhere in the world," Witkin explained, "and he's ready to assure Patterson that if he wins and becomes the heavyweight champion of the world, he's willing to post a substantial portion of his purse, under proper conditions, that he will fight Patterson a return match within a specified time. And for this first fight, he will fight under the promotion of any promoter selected by Patterson and/or his manager or his counsel."

"I've been dreaming about him three or four weeks," Liston revealed. "It seems like it's hard for us to get together, and then we're signing the contract, and then I wake up and it's just like a dream. I've never had a thing like this on my mind!"

Meanwhile, as usual, there were other problems.

For one thing, Liston and Katz weren't hitting it off smoothly. For another, the National Boxing Association was erecting blocks in its own patented obstacle course. Sometimes it seemed that Jack Johnson and Harry Wills had an easier time of it than Sonny Liston. An easier chase after the champion, that is.

Liston, who'd gotten very angry with Frank Mitchell because Mitchell sent him to Detroit alone to fight Marty Marshall, was disappointed that Katz never bothered to telephone to find out how things were in Denver, while Sonny was visiting Father Murphy.

Also, Katz's personality grated on Liston's nerves.

As one man explained it, "If you put a thousand dollars on the table and told Katz, 'You can have this or your picture in the paper,' Georgie wouldn't hesitate. He'd take his picture in the paper!"

This man recalled a time when he and Katz were walking along the boardwalk at Atlantic City and Katz was saying, loudly:

"The fight's gotta come. I'll make a champ outta the bum. I had Gil Turner . . ."

The man talking—and he happened to be Jack Nilon, who succeeded Katz as Liston's adviser or manager of record—concluded:

"I dropped back. I didn't want to be with him. I was embarrassed. In another world? He's in orbit! He's too much!"

Sports Illustrated observed that "none of this set well with Liston, who has an ego of his own. Contrary to some reports . . . Sonny is not a yea-saying Uncle Tom who can be led by the nose."

Sonny complained that Katz would "get on edge when I got on edge." With Liston, Katz was a 10 percenter. Once, when Liston was going to court on a Philadelphia charge, he asked Witkin: "Can I get the chair for this?" Witkin, startled, assured him seriously that he couldn't get the chair. "If I get the chair," Liston continued unsmilingly, "can I arrange for Katz to get 10 percent of the juice?"

In January, 1962, the National Boxing Association named Gene Fullmer as its "Fighter of the Year" and challenged its own president, Dr. Charles P. Larson, by again ranking Sonny Liston as the No. 1 heavyweight contender. During the previous month, Dr. Larson, of Tacoma, Washington, had denounced the reinstatement of Liston at the top after seven months of inactivity because of two embroilments with the law in Philadelphia. Larson said that Liston should have been forced to fight some ranking opponent, after his inactivity, to prove himself top contender.

It was interesting to note who the ranking fighters below Liston were: Eddie Machen, whom Sonny had beaten in a fistic track meet, with Machen running for his life; Alejandro Lavorante of Argentina, a tragically inexperienced fighter whom West Coast figures were then building up to knockouts by Archie Moore, Cassius Clay and one Jimmy Riggins, whose punch induced a months-long coma for Lavorante; Zora Folley, whom Liston had demolished; and Ingemar Johansson, whom Patterson had twice destroyed in return matches.

But after challenging Dr. Larson with its pro-Liston rating, the National Boxing Association's executive committee later in January gave Patterson a ninety-day extension of time from March 15 to June 15 in which to sign for a title defense [the National Boxing Association has a much-flaunted rule saying that title defenses must be made within a certain period of time]. Not only that, the National Boxing Association planned to stipulate only that Patterson defend against a "satisfactory challenger," not necessarily Liston. "Given 90 days," said Al Buck, "cautious Cus D'Amato, the careful champion's manager, is capable of digging up another Tom McNeeley, Jr., to be destroyed."

Yet Patterson, at the same time, was embarking on what was to seem like a fine pro-Liston publicity campaign. Once Patterson had decided that he would fight Liston, and had made known his decision publicly, he, himself, began "cleaning Liston up," with statements like these:

"Sometimes, many of us get off to a bad start. Liston has paid for his crimes. I met him at a boxing writers' dinner and I think he has a lot of good qualities buried within him. Should he be able to win the championship, these qualities will rise to the surface. I think you'd see a completely new and changed Liston."

In February, Admiral John J. Bergen, head of Madison Square Garden in New York, predicted that Liston and Patterson would fight in June in the new stadium at Washington, D.C. "There is every indication Patterson now makes his own decisions and that he is tired of fighting inconsequentials. A fight with Liston undoubtedly would draw big in New York, but the Championship Sports, Inc., outfit has picked the Capital. Conceivably it could make a fine deal for use of the arena which the Federal government has constructed for the baseball Senators and the football Redskins. I believe there is a general inclination to overrate Liston. *I think Patterson will knock him out.*"

But, actually the semi-secret plan was for Patterson to fight Liston in New York in June. There was dissension in the hallowed halls of Floyd Patterson Enterprises. D'Amato was against a bout with Liston. Julius November, Floyd's lawyer, was, however, in favor of the bout. Patterson sided with November.

"I'm a man," said Patterson, admitting that Liston was getting to him with his "fright" line. "Any man can say he'll beat me, but no man can say I'm afraid of him."

Patterson got in another publicity shot for Liston, too.

"He has paid for his shortcomings. They tell me he carries himself like a tough guy. But maybe that's because he had no education. He's had a pretty tough life. I think Liston will realize *the responsibility he has to the boys of America if he wins the championship.*"

Liston had by this time dropped Katz and taken on Jack Nilon, a Philadelphia food concessionaire, as his manager-of-record or adviser. A report had said D'Amato had okayed Nilon but D'Amato snorted a rebuttal: "There's no change—whether it's Nilon, rayon, cotton or silk." Someone explained that Nilon was a church-going Catholic, whereupon D'Amato blasphemed: "I don't give a damn if he was the Pope!" D'Amato didn't seem to approve of Nilon because he was, like Katz, a Philadelphian. "Philadelphia people are always considered [for Liston's management]," D'Amato complained. "This is a peculiar thing. Are there no other people? It could be Chicago, Los Angeles, New York. Why only Philadelphia people? As far as I'm concerned, I see no change in the situation and see no reason to change my opposition to the fight."

D'Amato, like Patterson already, was curiously to soften his blows at Liston once the fight was set for Chicago, where it was eventually held after the chase was drawn out even longer by New York's refusal to sanction the bout for that city in June, as planned over D'Amato's aching body.

Liston never let up his own campaign. He took advantage of every opportunity given by the press to make his point. He drummed it consistently, with a heavy beat, like the thud of his fists on Floyd Patterson's head and body on the night of September 25, 1962.

"I'll do anything to get that title fight with Patterson," he said once. "What do I have to do to get it?"

Referring to his rehabilitation, he said:

"I'm trying.

"It's already helped me in at least one way.

"Now, when I meet people, I don't feel so self-conscious. When I have to make a speech, the words don't come so hard. Once in a while, I even come up with a wisecrack that makes the people laugh.

"But, then, I think to myself, what has this all got to do with getting a shot at Patterson? The way I see it, the champion is supposed to fight the No. 1 contender. Well, I'm the No. 1 contender. So when are we going to fight?"

Things began to break Liston's way the latter part of February— or so it seemed. Patterson said he was ready to sign for the bout. Himself a marvelous example of a rehabilitated ex-juvenile delinquent, Patterson was attending an NAACP meeting in Jackson, Mississippi, at the time the National Boxing Association's executive committee met in New York and ordered him to enter into an agreement stipulating a title defense, though not necessarily against Liston, on or before March 15.

Patterson agreed publicly that Liston was the No. 1 contender. "I expect it will be the toughest fight of my career, if and when I fight Liston."

"I think we'll sign next week," Liston said on February 26. "Everything is just about set for a summer fight. I don't know where and I don't care where, just as long as I finally get him in a ring." But, a few days later, Liston changed his mind, and voiced disgust with the proffered terms, though he had said once that he would fight Patterson for nothing, just to get a chance at the title, if he had to.

Championship Sports, Inc., had offered Liston 12½ percent of the live gate and 10 percent of the ancillary rights (television, radio, movies, and so on) while Patterson, according to Liston, was to be paid 55 percent. Tom Bolan said Liston had refused 12½ percent of the gate, 12½ percent of the ancillary rights, and a minimum guarantee of $200,000.

"It's ridiculous," Liston said. "It appears they are trying to rob me blind. The others got 20 percent. Why not me?"

Liston also objected to Patterson's right to dictate terms for their rematch.

"I don't mind a 30–30 split for the second fight, with Bolan getting 40 percent," Liston said. "But they want to control the return fight in the same way as the first. They want to name the site, promoter, everything."

But hadn't he said he was so anxious to meet Patterson he'd fight for nothing?

"I said I'd fight him for nothing in the gym. But if a million people are watching, I want to get paid."

Julius November had a comment:

"I've never heard of a challenger being offered that kind of guarantee for a title fight. On the percentages, he stands to make more than $400,000. He sure could. Since when does the challenger dictate the terms to a champion?"

Liston had a strong point (which was to avail him nothing in the financial brawl with Floyd Patterson, Championship Sports, Inc., Julius November, et al). A 40–20 split for champion and challenger was the usual arrangement but there had been exceptions. Fullmer, for example, received only 12½ percent when he fought Sugar Ray Robinson in 1957.

The National Boxing Association refused to take action in the dispute.

Paul Sullivan, chairman of the National Boxing Association's championship committee, said that if there was an indication that either Patterson or the promoters were attempting to squeeze Liston

146

out of the title picture, then the National Boxing Association would consider the matter. But, said Sullivan, "that 12½ percent and $200,000 offer certainly do not give any indication of a squeeze play by Patterson."

On the contrary, Tom Bolan said, "this guarantee would make Liston the highest-paid first-time challenger in boxing history. Many challengers have been willing to fight for 10 percent or much less to get an opportunity to win the title." Bolan said he expected to reach an agreement with Liston but suggested that persistence on Liston's part in this financial argument could hurt his chances of meeting Patterson in a title bout.

"I know Patterson wouldn't want anyone to fight for nothing," said November, "or anything like nothing. But the fact remains that a smaller percentage of the great potential of this fight would be much greater in dollars than the 20 percent Liston refers to about other fights."

Speculation was that—at 12½ and 10 percent— Liston would gross four hundred and twenty-five thousand dollars of a total gate of four million dollars. It was pointed out that this amounted to more than five times his previous top purse, the seventy-five thousand dollars he received for the Westphal fight. The big emphasis was on *how much* money Liston would be making in dollars, not whether or not Liston was being offered a fair break in the percentages. And the situation subsequently proved ludicrous. Patterson had his way in the financial brawl, got himself knocked out in the first round, but, despite his pitiful showing, still maintained an equal financial break for the rematch with additional contractual powers of naming the site, and so on.

By all odds, this was a rather rough lesson for a man to whom the world was preaching morals! Legal or not, right or not according to business practices, it was a rough lesson!

This financial brawl didn't last long, though.

Bristling at the inference that Patterson was getting all the money, D'Amato issued another staccato remark: "Patterson gets what he gets and the other man is entitled to whatever he can get."

Liston decided, after three or four days, that he'd take whatever he could get.

With Witkin by his side, a rather tired and dubious looking Liston acquiesced. The lawyer did the talking.

"Let's make our position clear. We are not going to give any 'out' to Floyd Patterson.

"He is the heavyweight champion of the world. Sonny Liston wants that title. Sonny Liston will fight for it, and Sonny Liston expects to get it in June.

"We find no fault with his (Patterson's) endeavoring to get Sonny Liston as cheap as he can. We trust that no one can find fault with our trying to get for Sonny Liston what we think he demands."

In his own statement of capitulation, Liston said:

"I don't care where or how much, just as long as we fight."

Bolan was pleased. He said he'd speak to Patterson. Sonny Liston and Floyd Patterson signed a lengthy contract calling for their meeting in a world's heavyweight championship fight in the Embassy Ballroom of the Summit Hotel, New York City, on March 16, 1962.

From its offices in the hotel, Championship Sports, Inc., released this official statement:

"At today's signing of the contract between Floyd Patterson and Sonny Liston for a world's heavyweight championship match, Thomas A. Bolan, president of Championship Sports, announced the following terms and conditions of the agreement:

"1. On or before April 16, 1962, Patterson will designate the date and place of the match. The date of the match will be no earlier than June 18, 1962, and no later than September 30, 1962.

"2. Patterson will receive 55 percent of the proceeds from the sale of the ancillary rights and 45 percent of the live gate. Liston will receive 12½ percent of the ancillary rights and 12½ percent of the live gate, and a $200,000 guarantee.

"3. Championship Sports will promote the match and will receive 42½ percent of the live gate and 32½ of the ancillary rights."

4. Should Liston win the match, there will be a rematch no earlier than September 1, 1962, and no later than September 30, 1963. Patterson will decide the date, place and promoter of the rematch. Liston will receive 30 percent of the ancillary rights and 30 percent of the live gate for any rematch. No percentages are specified for either Patterson or the promoter of the rematch.

"Bolan stated that Patterson has authorized Championship Sports, Inc., to visit various cities and to explore all possibilities as to what would be the best site for the match and particularly to see what guarantees can be obtained. He stated that at least five cities were now under consideration. Bolan said that he would go abroad on Saturday and that in his absence his brother, Al Bolan, vice-president of Championship Sports, Inc., would visit different cities and obtain offers for the match.

"Bolan said that the fight would be carried over closed circuit theatre television and the rights to the same would be sold to the highest bidder. He stated that sealed bids would be accepted on a date to be announced."

Release of this official statement revealed this interesting fact: Championship Sports, Inc., not Patterson *per se*, was cutting into the percentages normally to be expected for Liston. Patterson and Championship Sports, Inc., certainly to be regarded as a tandem, since Patterson controlled the title and presumably made the major decisions, were taking 87½ percent of the live gate and ancillary rights and "leaving" Liston 12½. Although he was one-half of the performing cast and, certainly, the major creator of interest in the bout, he was merely going along for the ride, percentagewise.

Morals! Teach the man about morals!

Although it was an open secret that New York was to be the selected site—nobody thought otherwise— there was this talk about considering other cities—a procedure said to be good publicity and promotion practice. During the signing ceremonies and after, certain interesting statements were made!

"I was publicly opposed to Liston as a challenger and I have not changed my position now," said D'Amato. "Floyd Patterson wants this fight."

149

"*Sonny Liston was never asked to remove any obstacles,*" Morton Witkin said. "*He has not done anything.*"

"Obstacles?" Liston repeated. "That makes me think of Cus D'Amato."

Did Patterson think he'd win?

"Of course you expect to win," Patterson said in that inconclusive way of his. "A man must enter the ring with confidence."

"My intention," said Liston, "is to change his mind after three or four rounds . . . There's nobody in the world better than I am."

In order for Liston to fight Patterson in New York, he had one more important obstacle to hurdle. In a literal sense, he stumbled over it and fell. He needed a New York license. He didn't get it.

When Liston went to New York to apply for the license on April 17, 1962, it was already known that New York was the preferred site. By now, Championship Sports, Inc., had announced that the bout would be held at Yankee Stadium on September 17 or the Polo Grounds on September 26. Philadelphia, it was said, was a "possibility" for either of the two dates. All the other publicity-pawned cities were out of the running. If New York would take it, that is; which New York didn't.

The New York State Athletic Commission examined Liston thoroughly. He was given the same treatment any other fighter might expect, with "no special consideration." Dan Dowd, a deputy commissioner, interviewed Liston three-quarters of an hour. Dr. Samuel Swetnich's physical examination, including tests of the brain, heart, and chest, lasted an hour and forty-five minutes. By the time Liston had completed the process, virtually three hours were gone.

Nattily dressed and "all business," as one observer noted, Liston had only one touchy moment. Two photographers wanted to take pictures while he was being fingerprinted—a normal procedure—but they were successfully urged to forget it by Witkin and Harold Conrad, the Championship Sports, Inc., public relations director.

Sonny was somewhat testy about Patterson's failure to name the exact date of the fight.

"If a man's going to the electric chair," he said sarcastically, "he likes to put it off as long as he can."

But Liston maintained his normal prediction of the outcome . . . he picked himself, by a knockout, of course.

Normally, ten days elapse before the New York State Athletic Commission reports on an application for a license. "It takes that long for fingerprints to be processed in Albany," one commissioner explained. There were reports of some pressure on the commissioners to make a quicker decision—Liston had never fought in New York previously—but they weren't to be hurried. In the meantime, Witkin expressed confidence that Sonny would be licensed.

"I don't see why he should not be licensed," Witkin said. "It doesn't make any difference to Liston where the fight is held. All he wants to do is fight."

But . . . at this time, boxing was at a low ebb in New York. Liston himself was controversial. The great stir following Benny Paret's death compounded the tension, the pressure the commissioners labored under as they considered Sonny's application for a license.

Paret, a Cuban, had been beaten unmercifully by Emile Griffith in a New York ring on March 24. This was a title match. On April 2, Paret died of injuries suffered in this bout. An entire nation of television fight fans, as well as the live audience, had witnessed the brutal bout, which left Paret all but dead before their eyes, and the outcry against boxing had assumed worldwide proportions.

On April 27, the New York State Athletic Commission denied Liston a license to fight in that state. While composing their refusal, the commissioners cited Liston's criminal record and "his association with persons of unsavory background." A new box score of Liston's arrests and convictions was run up for all to read again, lest it had been forgotten.

The decision, hailed by some, came as a surprise to many.

Al Bolan said, "We didn't expect this decision because it's a deviation from the Commission's rules to the extent that Liston is licensed in other states and should be here. We'll be ready in a few days to settle where the bout will be staged."

151

November suggested that, since New York had refused to license Liston, perhaps the contract between him and Patterson was technically void. Jack Nilon's retort to that was, "Ridiculous!" He said that nothing in the contract stipulated that the bout had to be held in New York or that the agreement hinged on New York's decision.

Apparently surprised, if not shocked, by the news, Patterson expressed tremendous sympathy for Liston.

"He has already served his time," Floyd said. "What if they did that to me? You know how many times I went to the police station when I was nine years old? About a dozen. I used to steal from fruit stores and what not, but they've forgotten all about that. I feel sorry for him."

In fact, Patterson had far more to say about New York's denial of Liston than Sonny himself. While D'Amato criticized Liston and his handlers for making the application without some assurance that it would be approved, Patterson took occasion to reminisce, and relate:

"One night in bed, I made up my mind. I knew if I'd want to sleep comfortably, I'd have to take on Liston, even though the NAACP and the Kefauver Committee didn't want me to take on the fight. Some people said, 'What if you lose and he wins? Then the colored people will suffer.'

"But maybe if Liston wins, he'll live up to the title. He may make people look up to him."

Patterson said the big losers were New York State tax people. (It had been predicted that the fight would gross $6 million.)

In the *New York Journal American*, writer Murray Robinson said "my hat's off today to Messrs. Melvin Krulewitch, James A. Farley, Jr., and Raymond J. Lee of the New York State Athletic Commission for turning down Sonny Liston's application for a boxing license. The Commission gained immeasurably in stature with this decision, realizing, as it had to, that barring Liston would drive the heavyweight title bout between him and Floyd Patterson out of New York." But, in the *New York World Telegram and Sun*, writer Joe Williams said, "The spectacle of boxing commissioners lined up on the side of the angels, hymn books reverently clasped, heads uplifted in non-partisan spirituals, is so extraordinary, one stares in disbelief, reason becomes unhinged . . ."

Douglas Hayden, Chairman of the California Commission, sided with New York. But, in Los Angeles, promoter John Horn said: "I think Liston has paid his debt to society. I don't think he's any different than any other celebrity. The sporting public is going to demand that he be taken off probation. We have offered to back with $1 million the promotion here of a Liston-Patterson fight." Witkin said the New York decision was unfair, unjust, and un-American! Wilbert F. Lewis, Chairman of the Washington State Athletic Commission, said his group would look "very favorably" on the Liston-Patterson fight there. "The status of Sonny Liston hasn't changed since he fought Eddie Machen here two years ago," Lewis said. And, in Chicago, Commission Chairman Joseph Triner said:

"If they want to bring the fight to Chicago, they can rest assured that Sonny Liston will be given the right. I'm a firm believer in rehabilitation."

Not every Chicagoan shared Triner's view. In fact, by an odd twist of circumstances, or an odd consistency in circumstances, some of the same people who had opposed the Joe Louis-Jim Braddock heavyweight title bout now shot in their early licks against the Liston-Patterson fight.

But, while the controversy raged, Liston kept cool.

"I'm not concerned with the New York decision," he said. "I have full confidence in my attorney, Mort Witkin, and Jack Nilon, my adviser, who will become my manager in the future. I will continue to train as if nothing had happened."

"Offer you for your fighter Harold Johnson chance to fight for world heavyweight championship against Floyd Patterson here in Los Angeles in September. Open for negotiations."
—Joe Louis, in a telegram to George Gainford, on behalf of light heavyweight champion Harold Johnson, shortly after New York turned Liston down.

CHAPTER XV

Almost tragic in their aspect, the "shenanigans" of Sonny Liston's chase after Floyd Patterson become comical in retrospect.

While Patterson presumably pondered the choice of a second site, the story mills rolled. It was a good time for Jimmy Durante, or whoever said it, to say, "Everybody wants to get into the act." The wire reproduced above was purportedly sent to George Gainford in an "effort" to set up a Johnson-Patterson bout although, at the same time, Patterson was saying he'd quit fighting—"I'll never pull on another glove . . ."—if he couldn't meet Liston.

Just as nearly everybody had guessed right on New York the first time—as the planned site of the fight— now it was a secret as open as all outdoors that Chicago was ninety-nine to one to get the bout, now that New York had refused it.

But the game played on.

In Chicago on April 28, Joe Kellman, a rich glass manufacturer and former promoter of small-club fights, offered to stage the Liston-Patterson match in that city, provided Patterson would join him in giving half the proceeds to Kellman's favorite charity, the Better Boys Foundation.

Irv Schoenwald, well known in Chicago boxing circles, said Al Bolan had contacted him regarding rental fees and the availability of Comiskey Park and Soldier's Field between September 24 and 27.

Liston and Nilon reportedly were making a pitch for Philadelphia. But Patterson's comment was: "Philadelphia is definitely out. They'd do anything in that town."

D'Amato, meanwhile, was said to be "investigating" Chicago, Dallas, Houston, Washington, D.C., Seattle. Only the Taj Mahal was omitted from his itinerary. The possibility of a new contract between Liston and Patterson was scouted. But as Liston settled down in country-club style at South Fallsburgh, New York, Nilon said:

"The contract must be valid or we wouldn't waste our time and money going into training. There is nothing in there that says the fight is predicated on Sonny's being granted a license in New York."

Milton Gross, the New York writer who collaborated with Patterson on his book, *Victory Over Myself,* the publication of which had something to do with Patterson's choice of dates originally, said "a new contract will have to be signed."

Patterson said, "There will have to be a new contract signed, but it can have exactly the same terms in it as the other one. I don't want the contract voided, but Liston and his people had better not get the idea I'll give up anything in the new contract. If their attitude remains the same, we'll proceed with the same enthusiasm and conditions. If their attitude changes, then I'll have to change my attitude."

"I don't care where we fight," Liston said in South Fallsburgh. "I don't feel bad about New York turning me down, not after other states showed they wanted me. I would just like to fight.

"We have our biggest problem getting a place to fight. Once Patterson steps between the ropes, nobody can cut the ropes."

Liston added:

156

"I was not surprised that New York turned me down. The Philadelphia Commission told me, 'Don't be surprised if that happens.'"

Liston said it made him feel good to hear that Patterson had said that he would quit fighting unless he fought him. But, ironically, while Liston was speaking in this vein, somebody had told Patterson that Liston had said he'd knock him (Floyd) out in three or four rounds, and the then champion bristled again.

"Big men usually make big talk," Patterson said this time. "In the ring, it may be a little different." Then Patterson plied on more of his philosophy: "It's a strange thing about a person's outlook. When I meet a fighter at a weigh-in, or someplace else, like when I met Liston at the boxing writers' dinner, they seem to me to be twice my size. Then, when I get in the ring with them, I feel twice their size. I've had that happen to me since my amateur days. It's always the same. Liston can say anything he wants but he's not going to scare me. Talk is cheap and means nothing. What happens in the ring is what counts. We'll see then."

A bit later, from Highland Mills, New York, where he was training, Patterson said that only D'Amato was "authorized" to select a site for the September title bout.

"I want to make this clear in order to avoid confusion," Patterson said. "I've been surprised by newspaper stories about persons in many cities negotiating for the fight with people whom I have not authorized to negotiate." Patterson said he knew of four cities D'Amato had been negotiating with: "Kansas City, Baltimore, Houston, and Washington, D.C. . . . there may be one or two more. Cus and I will sit down early next week and choose the city that seems best for the fight. About ten days later, the site will be announced— after everything is wrapped up, so there can be no misunderstanding."

Another million-dollar offer for the bout came from a Chicago hotelman.

London promoter Jack Solomons said he was bidding for the bout.

Andy Frain, head of a Chicago ushering service, who had been working closely with Championship Sports, Inc., said he "felt sure" the bout was coming to Chicago.

On May 10, Leo Fischer, sports editor of the Chicago American, predicted in an exclusive story that "Floyd Patterson vs. Sonny Liston for the world's heavyweight boxing championship at Soldier's Field, September 17 or 18! Any day soon the official announcement will be forthcoming, barring unforeseen developments . . ."

But Floyd Patterson hadn't yet handed out the official word—for publication.

On the same day Fischer's story appeared in Chicago, D'Amato said in New York that Chicago had been eliminated from consideration because "as of this time . . . we haven't heard a word about a guarantee . . ."

The "word" came on May 23. The official word from the official man. Floyd Patterson announced that he would defend his title against Sonny Liston at Chicago sometime in September.

A basketful of details were yet to be worked out. But that was it.

"We have nothing to investigate as far as Liston is concerned."
—Joe Triner, Chairman, Illinois State Athletic Commission.

CHAPTER XVI

When the wheels started spinning in favor of Chicago as the site of the Liston-Patterson championship match, they kept on producing "pay-offs" until the final deed of Liston's knockout of Patterson was accomplished.

On the morning of May 24, while discussing the Chicago situation, Al Bolan said: "Only a couple things have to be ironed out, and we anticipate no difficulty."

None of the "things to be ironed out" had any bearing on a license for Sonny Liston. Joe Triner, Chairman of the Illinois State Athletic Commission, made this clear when he said, "We have nothing to investigate as far as Liston is concerned." Liston had been licensed earlier for an exhibition, and nothing had changed his status, insofar as this Commission was involved. There was some question as to who Liston's manager was—George Katz was the last manager registered in Chicago but Jack Nilon informed one and all that he'd taken over and "there is no more funny business" in the life of the heavyweight contender, he said. Nilon, then, needed a license, but this seemed to be a small formality.

Fact is, according to Bolan, the things to take care of immediately were the naming of a local promoter (Illinois law required this) and the choice of a site. Comiskey Park was, of course, the final choice, but not until after tours of other spots had been made, various finances had been discussed, and each move had been duly publicized.

There was also a small matter of setting up an Illinois corporation. This was solved in good time. Irv Schoenwald, a well-known Chicago promoter, fulfilled the Illinois requirement for a local participant in the staging of the bout.

From the beginning, it was determined that top priced tickets would sell for a hundred dollars [and this in spite of a few squawks heard around the town]. Bolan said:

"The people I've talked to here say they'd be offended if we have a lower top than a hundred dollars. That's the big-league rate, they say, and Chicago's big league."

Bolan didn't say whom he had been talking to.

At this point, two once hopeful promoters in Detroit were disgruntled, feeling that they had been "used" by D'Amato on his tour ostensibly to consider various sites. Michigan had voted to grant Liston a license and Elisha Gray and Leon Saddler had stepped up as prospective promoters. But they became angered when they learned that D'Amato had purportedly told David Gudelsky of the Michigan Boxing Commission that he (D'Amato) had little faith in their ability to produce a seven hundred and fifty thousand dollar guarantee. Saddler and Gray said D'Amato had been taking them for fools when he decided that they should put the fight on "in civic spirit . . ."

"I've got civic pride and a sense of civic duty," Saddler said, "but I don't have enough civic pride or foolishness to put up seven hundred and fifty thousand dollars and expect to get nothing in return."

In Chicago, meanwhile, Bolan said:

"We never intended to pit city against city in trying to get a better deal somewhere else. Why, we're not even asking for a guarantee in Chicago."

Bolan said the promotional group would be happy with a live gate of seven hundred and fifty thousand dollars.

"If we hit that figure," he said, "we'd know that we had selected the right place. However, I've heard estimates as high as $2 million from very reliable people." Triner estimated the bout would "do" between seven hundred and fifty thousand dollars and a million dollars.

Bolan said that Patterson and Julius November were "very happy with the situation. Chicago has been our first choice all along, but we just had to work out some difficulties."

The suspense of a fight that was to last only two minutes, six seconds, was built over a period of four months, during which all the publicity stops were pulled out, and millions of words, pro and con, were written.

Not a day passed between the time the bout was finally set and the night of the fight itself that the fan didn't find available to him mountains of "good copy." The controversy over Liston as a fit challenger was, of course, bandied about numerous times. But there were all sorts of angles besides that one.

The reader may discern, for future use, some of the "fine points" of fight promotion, as well as more about the subject of this book, in the following narrative.

Opening odds on the fight favored Liston, seven to five. And at no time did Patterson upset this betting pattern. Being a favorite was nothing new for Liston; he'd been the favorite in all of his major fights. Patterson, however, had been the underdog in two of his major bouts. Archie Moore was seven and one half to five over him and Ingemar Johansson was eight to five over him in their middle fight.

But there was a slight "taint" to Liston's favoritism, as expressed to writer Wendell Smith by a La Salle Street (Chicago) "broker."

". . . an aura of suspicion surrounds the people sponsoring Liston," he said. "No one questions Liston's ability as a fighter. The fact that he is the early favorite indicates that, but they are wary of his connections.

"No one is suspicious of Patterson. He is, and justifiably so, considered an 'untouchable.' But Liston's previous associations automatically throw a shadow of doubt around him, if he enters the fight the underdog."

Smith said, "Because of the heavy betting that is anticipated, as well as Liston's cloak-and-dagger background, the selection of the referee and judges for the September bout is of paramount interest."

One of the most interesting aspects of the "build-up" for the fight was the role Floyd Patterson played, one which, in fact, he had already indicated. That was the role of the opponent—"press agent." This was not entirely new, if new at all, in the fight game. Virtually all of those fellows who participated actively in Joe Louis' "Bum-of-the-Month" campaigns were described, at one time or the other, as being pugilists who might land that lucky punch, upset the dope and cart off the crown.

Patterson had established, and he maintained, this line of reasoning:

"Sonny has paid for whatever he did. He is entitled to help. There's no telling how I would have turned out myself if I hadn't been helped.

"One of those who expressed respect for Patterson because of this was the loser, Tom McNeeley, who said:

"I respect Floyd for insisting on fighting Sonny after the New York Commission gave him an out by refusing to license Liston. Floyd is that sort of guy."

Obviously, too, Patterson wasn't doing injury to his own reputation by taking the pro-Liston line which, in retrospect, and aside from publicity, probably was the only reasonable line he could take. He didn't have to, though. Hence the legitimate credit.

Early in June, Irv Schoenwald announced that fifty thousand dollars' worth of tickets had been sold. "I've never seen such a demand for tickets. I've got orders for exactly 459 tickets at $100 each, and I don't know how many other orders I have."

Another interesting—and usual—part of the build-up was the collection of testimonials from other fighters. Some got their votes in early.

Billy Soose, a former middleweight champion called the "Poet of the Poconos," predicted that Patterson would knock out Liston, expounding:

"Boxing is dead enough now. Television has it leaning over the coffin and if a man of Liston's background should win and fail to walk with extreme caution, that might be the coup de grace."

Billy Conn, who'd once electrified the boxing world with his tremendous stand against Joe Louis, picked Liston because "he's tough and Patterson can be hit so easily. He even acts like he expects it. I don't see how he can keep away from Liston."

In the long run of the build-up, Jack Dempsey was quoted both ways. But, at one time, he said: "If Patterson can land often with his jab, and keep moving, Liston will be just another guy with a big mouth who didn't make it."

Louis, whose record as a "tout" was rather poor, picked Liston, saying: "I wouldn't want to have to pick between them, but I've got my money on Liston. Floyd has fast hands but somewhere Liston is gonna catch him. He's got the power and I like to go with the puncher." Louis stuck with this prediction to the end . . . when, of course, he was proven right.

Lou Viscusi, manager of heavyweight Cleveland Williams, recalled that "Williams was doing fine until Liston started popping him with that left. Once he started connecting with it, my guy, who moves pretty fast, had no chance."

The first time Cleveland was knocked out in the third round. He lasted only two the second time. Patterson probably will have just as much trouble escaping the left. It's unescapable, believe me, and the worst thing about it is that it's the kind of punch that hurts. I'd say it's the best left hand in the heavyweight division since Louis was champion."

Pete Rademacher, who made his debut as a professional in an ill-fated venture at Seattle, said: "Patterson will be ahead on points up to the time Liston knocks him out."

In the middle of June, the promoters determined that Liston and Patterson should begin training in the Chicago area six weeks prior to the fight date—September 25.

Tom McNeeley not training in Toronto for his fight with Patterson hurt the gate," Al Bolan said. "We can't afford to repeat that mistake."

Less than a month later, Liston halted his training at South Fallsburgh, New York, because, he said, "I was shedding too much. Now I'm back to 225 pounds and feel great." He added, "Maybe I train too hard. This place has everything from wet and dry steam rooms to a golf course on which par seems a friend rather than an enemy. Maybe, I've been taking my work too seriously.

Three months before the fight, it was announced that ancillary rights, including television, radio and motion picture coverage, had been sold to the Los Angeles firm of Graff, Reiner and Smith Enterprises for a two-million-dollar guarantee.

On July 2, Liston and Patterson formally signed contracts for the heavyweight title bout at Chicago.

Quite a lot of dialogue was recorded from this press covered session.

"I've seen him fight twice," said Patterson, of Liston, "and he knocked out both of his opponents. That's the way I want to remember him." Patterson wanted to think of his opponent "as the best man I've ever fought." He went on, "I don't want any film of his fights that went the distance because maybe he didn't look too good, and I don't want to know about that.

"You've got to build up your viciousness for the fight. I don't see my family. I do a lot of sacrificing, and I hope to reach my peak for the fight."

Patterson was now boxing two or three times weekly, doing a lot of road work, punching both light and heavy bags.

"Staleness is more mental than physical," Floyd continued, "and you have to work to develop your mental attitude for a fight even more than your physical condition." Oddly, Patterson thought the odds against him were a boon to his chances of winning because "I've always done better as the underdog."

It was announced that the fighters would wear eight-ounce gloves and that, in case of knockdowns, the mandatory eight-count was in order.

"We think it's good insurance and eight ounces is light enough," Joe Triner said. "I think the mandatory eight-count is the best thing ever legislated in boxing." Liston wasn't nearly as voluble as Patterson, who thought the eight-ounce gloves and mandatory eight count ruled by Illinois for a title bout for the first time had something to do with the death of Benny Paret.

Liston said the rules were okay by him.

"I just want a referee who can count further than eight and not stop somewhere along the way," he said.

Sonny dismissed inquiries about his management by saying, "Me and Patterson are doing the fighting . . . not the managers."

A bit later, Sonny made a more learned analysis of the upcoming fight:

"Speed is really not important in this fight. If my timing is right, I'll have little trouble with Patterson. I'll catch him somewhere along the way. I don't think he can run away from me for 15 rounds. I am sure I can take his punches, but I doubt he can take mine."

Patterson, who was to develop what, on the surface, appeared to be modesty to a fine point of almost predicting doom for himself, applauded the safety measures instituted by the Illinois Commission: "I know the press won't agree with me but I believe in every precaution in a sporting event, whether it be boxing, football or anything else."

Floyd said this, as he said most everything, in a soft, articulate way, which *Esquire* magazine publisher Arnold Gingrich said was equal to the public speaking talents of some senators he'd heard.

Along about here, Archie Moore prophesied: "*Somebody's going to be humiliated so bad the public won't stand for another fight.*"

When Liston appeared in Chicago to participate in the Bud Billikin Day parade, a children's event sponsored annually by the *Chicago Daily Defender*, he mentioned the subject of Patterson's speed again.

"Patterson isn't as fast as some people think," he said. "He looks fast because most of his opponents have been slow. Ingemar Johansson was slow and so were opponents like Roy Harris and Pete Rademacher. I believe I'm faster than any fighter Patterson has faced since he won the title. I'm a big man but I'm not a slow one. I'll catch up with him somewhere along the way and expect to knock him out."

Liston added, "Williams was just as quick on his feet as Patterson and I caught up to him in two rounds and knocked him out. He not only was as fast as Floyd, but he hit harder."

Against the backdrop of our knowledge that Liston demolished Patterson easily when they met, the most amazing part of all this dialogue is the fact of Liston's unerring accuracy. Some called him a loudmouth and a braggart but, history proved, Liston told nothing but the truth, and the whole truth it was, about his forthcoming fight. Everything fell into place just as he said it would. His estimate of his own punch, his own speed, Patterson's punch, Patterson's vaunted speed, the lack of importance of glove weights, the importance of a referee capable of counting to ten, the predictions as to the length of the fight . . . every point Liston made was as true as the fact that God made little apples. Another point Liston made well, too, was encompassed by his appraisal of Patterson's previous opponents. Here, again, he was strictly on-target; he was not, like some chronic no-good, shilling the public, as the public has been shilled often by "reputable" people in many sports, and in show business, and in politics . . . for sure, in politics! But, of course, as we know, the people didn't want to believe this man they'd labeled a Nogoodnik when he came bearing the truth . . . just as, in a loose sort of analogy, nobody wanted to believe the fabled boy who wasn't lying the last time about that wolf. In regard to his boxing ability, as contrasted to Patterson's, Liston never lied once!

But Liston did soften one phase of his "attack" on Patterson. In reply to a question at Chicago, he said:

"I think he's a very nice fellow . . ."

Prior to the Patterson bout—which, of course, means never, as this is written—Liston hadn't gone more than twelve rounds in a fight (the Machen bout). For this one, he trained with all intentions of not going more than five rounds. As he repeated his standard line, in different words: "I never think about how a fight is going to go—but it won't go more than five rounds."

At South Fallsburgh, New York, he rounded into shape too quickly, necessitating a lay-off at home in Philadelphia. At the time, Liston was down to two hundred and twenty pounds. He predicted he'd "come in" at about two hundred and twelve.

Early in August, he selected his final training site, the defunct Aurora Downs race track, located twenty-eight miles southwest of Chicago. Patterson delayed his selection of a final training site before, finally, selecting a tranquil farm near Elgin, Illinois. And, compared to the camp Liston ran, with its near open-facedness, jazz music [Sonny skipped rope to the record, Night Train], and awesome physical performances, Patterson's place was a monastery.

A few days after Liston selected the Aurora Downs site, Roy Harris, who'd fought both Sonny and Floyd, thus enjoying the distinction of being their only common foe, spoke a few learned words for the benefit of the reading public. To call his words "learned" is not to be facetious, not by any means. Harris had learned a lot while fighting both of the title opponents and, moreover, he was a well-spoken former schoolteacher who was, by now, operating a ranch and studying law.

He had, for understandable reasons, retired from the ring.

"I was sure I could take Patterson that first time (we fought)," Harris said. "I'd been unbeaten in 22 fights; I'd solved every style I came up against. I had studied Floyd by watching half a dozen of his fights on TV.

"You know what happened—a TKO for Patterson at the end of 12. I had the satisfaction of putting him on the floor in the second

167

round, but he kept coming at me when he got up and he dropped me four times . . ."

What about Sonny Liston?

"I realized Sonny was a powerful puncher," Harris continued, "but he appeared to be slow and cumbersome and I was sure I had the speed, skill and experience to stay out of range.

"I didn't get much of a chance to use that speed, skill and experience. I started out by poking three or four left jabs in Liston's face. I guess that's where I made my mistake. I became careless—and the next thing I knew, I was under the lower rope and Referee Jimmy Webb was counting over me. Later, I was told that Liston had caught me with a left hook.

"I went down again, more from pushing than punching. The third time I hit the floor, I slipped and skidded. The fourth time I went down, I'd say, I was wrestled, not punched. I could have gotten up again, but the referee must have figured I'd only run into more trouble and maybe serious injury. The fight was stopped with about 25 seconds to go in the first round.

"I would give Floyd a good chance if I knew he would come in at 185 pounds or less. He can't afford to sacrifice by coming in anywhere near 195 for strength. With speed, Floyd can out-flurry Sonny and out-box him.

"But I have to go along with Sonny's ammunition. Sooner or later, he will catch Floyd. My guess is that it will be in six or seven rounds."

If there was any doubt that Liston was dead-serious about the title bout and quite anxious to be at-the-ready, this doubt was dispelled when he arrived at Aurora Downs, much to the surprise of the promoters, before the camp was ready.

"But, nevertheless, he's here," Al Bolan said, "and that is the most important thing."

"I will say," Sonny observed, just to keep the record straight, "that I'm the next heavyweight champion. I'll knock Patterson out."

Meanwhile, Patterson was still training at Highland Mills and providing ample copy for sports writers.

"This is another proving fight for me," he said. "I've had something to prove in a lot of my fights—that I had a punch, for example. Apparently, a lot of people are still unconvinced. Maybe I can convince them if I beat Liston."

In another appraisal of Liston, the fighter, he said: "Well . . . he's got the strength and durability and punch to be champion. They say he's a bit slow, but when you've got all the other things he's got, that might not make any difference."

He had more to say about Liston, the man:

"I think he's paid his debts. And his friends are probably the same ones he had when no one else would be his friend. Mostly, I don't think it's fair that they let him climb all the way up to number one contender, then try to keep him from fighting for the title. He deserves the chance."

At another time, Patterson said, "If Liston should be fortunate to win the title, I hope you will accept him the way you've accepted me. You know, there's a little good in everybody."

It was significant, though not properly appraised at the time, that Patterson often prefaced his own declarations of impending personal victory by using the phrase . . . "If I should be fortunate . . ." Overlooked in all of the pre-fight publicity, too, was the fact that, on one occasion sometime previously, Patterson had predicted that Sonny Liston would someday be the world's heavyweight champion!

Red Smith, who—possibly excepting Jim Murray— had more journalistic fun than anyone while writing about this title fight, made a pertinent point in one of his widely read columns.

"If Cus [D'Amato] is a competent judge of ability," Smith wrote, "then his reluctance to send Patterson in against Liston could be significant. The lofty principles which Cus so frequently attributes to himself would not have deterred him from taking a possible $4,000,000 match if he considered it a soft touch. At those prices, he would have heard a divine call to punish Liston for his sins. . . ."

Regardless of what Patterson thought privately about the upcoming fight, or his own chances, he obviously wanted to make sure that many of his friends saw the bout. Presumably, at least, that's why he personally ordered twelve thousand five hundred dollars' worth of one-hundred-dollar ringside seats.

At Aurora Downs, Liston established two rules which were, more or less, observed religiously:

He would not answer any questions about his past personal life.

The press would be barred from interviews, except immediately after his daily workout.

One of those who attempted to violate rule No. 1 was "a fellow with a peg leg [who] ignored a 'Keep Out!' sign and walked right into Liston's dining room," writer Jimmy Breslin reported in the *Saturday Evening Post*.

"I know who he is," Sonny said. "I don't want to talk with him. I was in jail with him."

"Sonny, you remember me," the man said, approaching Liston. "I'm Louis. We went to school together. Remember?"

"Then I can't know you at all," Liston said. "I never went to school."

Liston's camp aides laughed. Louis persisted.

"Sonny," he said, "I'm fine. I'm working. I'm a registered voter . . . All I want is two tickets for the fight. I'm not asking for a hundred dollars."

"I don't think they're giving out any tickets for the fight," Liston told Louis.

Louis then whispered a few words into Liston's ear, whereupon, Breslin reported, Liston bridled. "Look," he ordered, "don't talk about that stuff. That's all behind me."

On August 21, Liston began serious training at Aurora Downs.

It was a rigorous performance, vastly impressive, too.

Weighing two hundred and twenty-four pounds, working to shed twelve or fourteen, Sonny opened the training day by running around the track.

Later he shadow-boxed three three-minute rounds, worked out on the heavy bag three additional rounds, skipped rope to the tune *Night Train*, then—startlingly!—allowed his trainers to hurl a twelve-pound medicine ball into his midriff more than a dozen times . . . to tone up the muscles!

To this regimen, later stepped up in the phases described above, Liston of course added sparring sessions.

When Patterson began his training at Marycrest Farm near Elgin, he said:

"If I have a worry about this fight, it is to make certain that I don't overtrain or arrive at my fighting peak too soon. That is why I intend regulating well every moment of my training grind, in the ring shadowboxing and the other exercises that I will engage in."

In an early sparring session at Marycrest, Patterson sparred six rounds with five different opponents, selected because they fought "Liston's style."

Speculating on the fact that he'd meet Liston with a disadvantage in weights, Patterson declared that "prize fighting is not like football. I won't be tackling him. I won't be wrestling him. I'll be skillfully boxing him."

He readily admitted that Liston was the heaviest man he'd ever fought but he minimized Sonny's weight advantage. He explained why there were no outstanding heavyweight fighters who weighed two hundred and thirty pounds or better:

"I know when I'm just a few pounds overweight that I slow down tremendously. Imagine how much slower a man would be if he weighed forty or fifty pounds more than I do."

Joe DiMaggio, the old Yankee Clipper, picked Liston to win.

"Floyd is smart, experienced, has good speed and can change pace in the ring," said the former home run slugger and long-time fight observer. "Liston is the slugger. He's always capable of taking out his opponent at any stage of the fight."

DiMaggio saw the bout as a classic, "sudden-death fight," between a pitcher and a hitter.

Liston was, of course, the hitter.

But Patterson was to be . . . not the pitcher . . . the catcher!

Graff, Reiner, and Smith Enterprises, Inc., was the firm selected by the promoters, et al., to handle the theatre telecast of the championship fight. The firm, like Championship Sports, Inc., maintained headquarters at the Sheraton-Chicago Hotel, replete with a director of public relations and a research and release director. In their August 23, 1962, release, with Harold Conrad handling the actual writing, they said:

"Popular opinion concerning Sonny Liston's effort to knock the heavyweight championship off the head of Floyd Patterson . . . is that the challenger will have to do it quickly—or not at all.

"There is evidence, however, that the rangy, mighty muscled No. 1 challenger has conditioned himself to win over the long haul. There also is reason to believe that he has the tools to win in a fight that might go the full fifteen rounds.

"Liston happens to be one of the most industrious road runners in boxing annals and the sturdiness of his legs are an essential towards carrying him the entire distance.

"Couple his stamina with his cruelly effective left jab and his own known capacity to take a punch—and there's a parlay that is certain to demand the best of Patterson in defense of his crown.

"That the name of the game with Liston is legs is comprehended by anyone who has witnessed one of his early morning workouts at camp. The first gesture after he leaves his quarters at the crack of dawn is not merely to start jogging. It's a ritual of limbering up which takes more than five minutes. He bows, he bends, he twists, he turns. He shadow boxes, he runs in place. He cracks a full sweat before he heads down the road.

"And, once he goes, the watcher is surprised to note that he quickly pulls ahead of his sparring partners, although they appear to be working harder than he does.

"Sonny has an odd, duck-footed gait which takes him over the ground at a surprising rate of speed.

"One of the points of departure in Liston's road running is that he likes to run on a railroad track. He feels that the space between the ties compels him to stretch his stride and 'unfreeze' his leg muscles.

"When he was working at South Fallsburgh, New York, Sonny found out there was an abandoned rail road near the camp and, the first morning he ran, he headed for the site. The trackage runs for about four hundred yards. He loped back and forth on the tracks, like a one-man shuttle relay team, obviously deriving satisfaction from the unique jaunt.

"But the track-running is only spice for Liston. He had several courses through the country roads which provided the bulk of his road work. One route took him three to three and a half miles. Another took him two and three-quarter miles. A third covered about two and a half.

"The middle-range route was almost entirely hills. It was on a golf course. And he seemed to relish this climbing routine. People watching him and his sparring partners run could see Sonny outdistancing his associates on the testing up-grade.

"The shortest course had its own compensation. This one went through some fields dotted with old, low fences, about two and a half feet high. Sonny converted this into a steeplechase course. And, again, his flexibility was demonstrated as he cleared the fences without breaking stride.

"His well-conditioned legs do not demand quick success. They are patient and persevering, as has been Liston in his quest for the title. They will go as far as need be."

Publicity, as you can see, doesn't always have to be a shill.

Willie Reddish, Liston's trainer, is a former heavyweight fighter who is not too well known outside Philadelphia, his hometown, yet he is recognized by fight men as a shrewd, forthright teacher and ring psychologist.

One of Reddish's strong points in the handling of Liston was his early understanding of the fact that it's easier to encourage Sonny than it is to command him. "I can get a lot out of Sonny by not asking too much," is the way Reddish explains his gift with the champion.

His "secret" method is to observe Sonny's moves "which accomplish the job in the long run but which can be improved by a short cut. He'll say to Sonny, 'Here's an easier way to do that.' Sonny will respond, 'You're right; I've been thinking there was a better way.'"

Following a one-hour workout on August 24, 1952, Liston told the press:

"If the fight is close, they can give it to Patterson. It won't be close. I don't think he will run from me—any champion should come out fighting. *I don't think he will get up once I hit him right.*"

Sixty people had watched the workout.

Frank Leahy, the former Notre Dame football coach, was on hand, supervising movie-making for a then proposed television show. Another witness was Father Murphy of Denver, Colorado.

During the workout, Liston toiled in steaming heat in his outdoor gym at Aurora Downs, caving in his eighty pound "big bag," taking the medicine ball in his belly a dozen times, skipping rope to three renditions of *Night Train*. Then he showered and met newsmen in the air-cooled clubhouse while sipping a cup of tea, smartened with a slice of lemon, sweetened with four teaspoons of sugar.

"I weighed two hundred and nineteen before the workout," Sonny said, "and lost six during it. I plan to fight him at something under two hundred and fifteen. Someone once said the bigger they are the harder they fall. I say the bigger the trees, the harder they are to cut down.

"If I'm not ready when the bell sounds, I won't be in there against him. If Sugar Ray Robinson didn't think he was ready for a fight, he'd pull a muscle or something and it would be postponed.

"If I win, I might fight Johansson. But, first, he must fight Cleveland Williams. There is a one-year return match in the Patterson fight, but my plan is to make him not want a return fight."

He added:

"I hear Johansson says I'm slow. I saw him fight Patterson twice. He was lucky. He should be locked up for impersonating a fighter.

"I went the full twelve rounds with Eddie Machen. It's the longest I ever went. It takes two to tango and Machen wasn't in the mood to. I don't think Patterson will run. I caught Machen and I don't think anybody can run as fast as him."

In a slight variance of this, Liston also said:

"I always press my opponent. He's got what I want and I got to go get it. I feel any champion should come out and fight like a champion. My plans are to make him not want a return bout, but if it's close, give it to him. I'm going for a knockout."

Martin W. Smith, President of Graff, Reiner, and Smith, Enterprises, Inc., predicted that more people would see Liston and Patterson in action than all those who'd seen all previous heavyweight title bouts dating back to John L. Sullivan.

Cus D'Amato showed up at Patterson's camp, to the surprise of some observers. On his arrival at Elgin, Illinois, Patterson had said he didn't know where Cus was, nor whether he'd come to camp. But Cus moved into quarters at Marycrest and said he'd be there through the fight.

During their workouts at Aurora Downs and Marycrest Farm, it was obvious that Liston and Patterson had different ideas about the rigorous training-camp routines.

Liston approached the drudgery of it with some distaste; he viewed it as a necessary evil.

Patterson, nearly always in training, somewhere or somehow, seemed more dedicated.

Liston's apparent distaste for training may have been, however, a pose. The fact was, drudgery or not, he never shirked it. He worked, as the saying goes, like a Trojan.

"He gives the air of a man who regards all this as nonsense," said one reporter of Liston. "This isn't the real thing and that's what Liston wants—the real thing, tonight, tomorrow or any time he can get Patterson in the ring with him.

"His face is emotionless when he comes into the ring at 2:30 P.M. . . . to punch the bag or to box with his sparring mates.

"If he is aware there is a crowd of spectators at ringside, he never shows it. His face never changes, his eyes seldom blink. About the only animation he shows is at the end of his afternoon workout when he does a rope skipping act to the tune of rock 'n' roll records.

"And then he displays an amazing agility for a man so large, and for the first time in the afternoon workout, some delight will come to his face."

United Press International teletyped a lengthy pre-fight story on August 28, 1962:

"If there's any vitality left in the American prizefight industry, Floyd Patterson and Sonny Liston figure to bring it out when they meet for the world heavyweight championship . . .

"But if this one's a box-office dud or an artistic flop, boxing is a cinch to get another major set-back and that's about as welcome as a Congressional investigation.

"All signs point to a success, however, and folks who retain an interest in boxing have the ingredients for a furious evening of fisticuffs.

"The fighters present a sharp contrast in styles, personalities, ring records, and, at least lately, out-of-the ring records.

"Furthermore, they're the only two heavyweights around who could draw much of a gate at any time or any place.

"It's a tough fight to pick and that factor never hurt a heavyweight gate.

"Patterson is the champ and there are guys who always go down the line with a titleholder. But Floyd also is a champ who lost the title once and he has the unhappy habit of being decked frequently by even the most ill-equipped fighters.

"Floyd revealed he is doing something to strengthen his chin and, presumably, something to stabilize his equilibrium so he won't go tumbling down the first time Sonny belts him.

"Yet, he still retains certain amateurish boxing habits that crop out when the going is heavy. And Liston, though bigger and slower, expects to keep the pressure heavy.

"Liston is a puncher who, like Ingemar Johansson, confidently expects to land a Sunday shot on Patterson's chin.

"'But when I hit him,' says Sonny, 'he'll stay down.'

"All through the negotiating and preliminary training, Liston has been saying things like that. Patterson, on the other hand, openly campaigned to have Liston accepted by the New York State Commission for a New York fight and was shocked when the Commission turned thumbs down because of Liston's brushes with the law.

"'He deserves the chance,' said Floyd.

"So Sonny will have it at Chicago, which quickly accepted the bout after the New York Commission turned it away.

"The heavyweight title may or may not regain some of its prestige if Liston becomes the champ. It hasn't meant much—except money—to any titleholder since Joe Louis.

"Ezzard Charles, Jersey Joe Walcott, Rocky Marciano, Patterson, Johansson, then Patterson never gained the general acclaim the heavy title always had carried in the past, before television saturation set in and boxing moved downhill.

"Liston, despite his personal history, might be quite a champ. Certainly he won't go into hiding as Patterson did and maybe he won't hand-pick future foes as carefully.

"But one way or another, Floyd and Sonny have a date that's important to the prize-fight industry as a whole. They have a chance to give it a shot in the arm."

They continued to ask questions.

Sonny Liston continued to supply answers.

Had he predicted he'd get Patterson in the fifth round?

"I said the fight wouldn't go as far as the fifth round."

Why are you so confident?

"I know myself."

Are you down-grading Patterson?

"Patterson is a very good fighter. I fought a very good fighter in Folley."

Is Folley a better fighter than Patterson?

"I don't know. I fought Folley; but I ain't fought Patterson."

Patterson, a pretty good press-agent, was talking, about Liston:

"Speed should be helpful against Liston. Speed should confuse him, style could confuse him and combinations could confuse him."

Arthur Daley of the *New York Times* found Aurora Downs to be a rather forlorn place. "But there's nothing ghostly about its present tenant. Liston is bigger than life." Daley was impressed by Sonny's high-powered glare. "It can fell a man at twenty paces, especially when loaded with resentment." Sonny's hello to Daley was a growl. His tone was surly. "No," Sonny said in response to a question as to whether he'd studied movies of Patterson's fights, "he wouldn't be fighting me in them, would he?"

Speed?

"I don't think I'm as slow as Johansson says," Liston said belligerently, as Daley reported it. "I don't think Patterson is so fast. He ain't no faster than me. It took him twelve rounds to catch up with Roy Harris. I knocked out Harris in the first. If Patterson is so fast, he picked up a lot of speed since then."

Did he (Liston) run the mile under four minutes?

"We don't go that fast."

As August came to an end, Patterson said:

"I don't care who everybody is picking . . . I pick me."

Meanwhile, in a sparring session, Liston staggered Foneda Cox with short, left hooks in the second and third rounds.

Pete Rademacher was watching.

178

Roy Harris enlarged what he'd said earlier into a *Ring* magazine article. Same conclusion. The winner: Liston.

"It will be the rapier against the bludgeon when Floyd Patterson defends his world heavyweight championship against Sonny Liston . . ." Arthur Daley said. "Interest in this intriguing duel keeps snowballing and differences of opinion as to the outcome will provoke more saloon arguments than any fight in recent memory."

Sonny Liston was angry on September 5. He was angry about the short end he was taking financially.

"I figure," he said, "Patterson put up that figure thinking I wouldn't take it, would turn it down. I hold him responsible."

Al Bolan said Patterson had nothing to do with it.

Sonny was still angry . . . it was said.

"He had to offer me some kind of proposition," said Sonny, "so he said he'd fight me if I'd take 12½ percent. He's taking 45 percent of everything.

"That's not much for me when you consider that the pushover challengers Patterson has defended against received anything from 20 percent upwards.

"I think Patterson figured I'd refuse to fight him for 12½. But I want that title so badly, I'd fight him for nothing."

More:

"I figure Patterson will try to come to me, to fight inside, and I think the kind of punches I was throwing in the drill will make him back away. He can't take these kind of punches and keep coming."

Still more:

"I don't hate Floyd but I certainly do not like him. I believe he could have given me a fairer percentage of the gate. I agreed to the deal because I know within myself I can beat him. I'm going to knock him out.

"I'll keep the pressure on him so strongly that he won't have a chance to lunge at me.

179

"You know how he flies off his feet when he makes that leaping lunge? Well, I'm not going to give him enough distance to do it.

"It's all a matter of timing. I'll time my punches so that when he leaps, I'll connect.

"I don't think this is going to be a long fight. I'll connect somewhere during the first five rounds and take the championship."

Willie Reddish was talking:

"No, I don't give him (Sonny) too much advice when a fight's on. I give him just what I see, just enough for him to remember. You don't want to tell a fighter too much when he's fighting . . .

"He's not hard to train. Other day, he came to me and he said, 'Will, I feel good.' So I know he's getting there.

"He fools you. He's so aware of what's going on.

"He sees things before other people can see them, or remembers things other people forget.

"We'll be walking along, and he'll say, 'Will, you see such-and-such, or you remember such-and-such?' and it's hard for me to remember.

"He deeply believes he's going to win . . . He and I'd be the most let-down people in the world if he didn't.

"We don't want to have too much confidence, but we believe he's going to knock out Floyd."

Somebody asked Sonny how he was going to fight Patterson.

"Like he's got a gun in his hand!"

Jack Dempsey, one of the two most-glorified of heavyweight champions, Joe Louis being the other, was talking:

"Liston is much bigger, stronger, more rugged and can take a punch. He may be slow on his feet, but he is fast with his punches.

"Patterson, on the other hand, is fast, can box and can hit. We know Patterson doesn't take a punch too well. But he has proved that when he's knocked down, he can get up.

180

"When the fight starts, Patterson may have to decide whether he wants to box Liston or slug it out with him. I personally think he has got to box Liston. He has to be in good shape and he has got to move. He may be able to cut up this fellow and then it may be a question of how much Liston can take."

Ezzard Charles, former heavyweight champion, picked Patterson. He thought all the talk about Floyd's weak chin had been "overplayed."

John Roxborough, a manager of Joe Louis, said: "I pick Liston to win this fight by a knockout. He can knock Floyd out with either hand, his right or left. I don't think Patterson hits hard enough to beat Liston, who takes a blow as well as he delivers one."

Scene: Sonny Liston's training camp in Aurora Downs.

Music is playing all the time. "Supposedly to soothe the animal instincts of the challenger," says a dramatist.

A man appears in view of the visiting fans and writers. He gives a resume of Liston's fighting record.

He says, "Please don't smoke . . . and last, but not least, Sonny married his childhood sweetheart, Geraldine, who is really the boss."

The music plays.

The man speaks: "Ladies and gentlemen, I am happy to introduce Sonny Liston, the No. 1 contender for the world's heavyweight title."

Liston enters.

He's wearing a white robe.

Emblazoned on the back of the robe are the words

"Sonny Liston" . . . and an emblem of a half-rising Sun.

Sonny begins shadow-boxing.

A sparring partner enters.

Sonny and the sparring partner shadow-box.

The sparring partner is the size of Floyd Patterson.

Liston shows his left. It's awfully fast.

Liston shows his right. It looks slow.

Two rounds go by.

Sonny never smiles.

Not until he unloads a double-left on his opponent.

The opponent is surprised, obviously. Sonny has scored.

Liston steps out of the ring.

The audience applauds.

Sonny gives the heavy bag hell.

The audience is awed.

He moves to the small bag.

It takes a beating, too. The sound is like a machine gun's firing.

Reddish eventually calls . . . "time!"

The record-player is set up.

Liston gets his rope.

The strains of *Night Train* blare forth.

Sonny skips . . . adroitly.

Night Train stops . . . and so does Sonny.

It plays out again.

Willie Reddish gets the medicine ball.

Willie heaves the ball into Sonny's midsection.

Sonny takes the blows of the ball without blinking, and catches the ball on the rebound (try it sometime).

The ball, you should know, weighs twelve pounds!

The crowd is amazed.

Willie Reddish is huffing and puffing—like he's going to blow a house in.

Liston is as calm as City Hall at night, when all the politicians have vacated.

He does sitting-up exercises.

He takes a massage from Reddish.

He finally puts on his robe . . . and walks away.

He's going to the showers.

That's it for the day!

Enters the ludicrous!

Its representative is Cus D'Amato, press-agent for Floyd Patterson and, therefore, this upcoming heavyweight title fight.

He's got a worry: it's possible to hypnotize a fighter and make him immune to pain.

He appears before the Illinois Boxing Commission. He's requested a hearing because he's discovered a letter written to Sonny Liston.

Jimmy Grippo, a former fight manager, is the author.

Grippo wants to work his hypnotic powers on Liston.

D'Amato wants the Commission to "outlaw" hypnotism because "if Sonny Liston was in the ring and under hypnosis he could break a hand and not know it was broken; he could be crippled for life."

This D'Amato bit came under the general heading of humanitarianism.

Yet South Side Chicagoans were known to complain about the smell of the stockyards of a summer when the wind was still and the heat was high.

Yet, of such stuff is pre-fight publicity made!

Cus had a description of Liston:

"He doesn't move away from you, he sort of moves around you, like he's going to wrap you up. He's cute and tricky."

Liston could be difficult:

"Sonny has the height and weight. He's stronger than Moore, I think, and faster than Johansson. *That's a tough combination to beat.*"

Red Smith said:

"Floyd Patterson is a thoroughly decent human being . . . .

"Sonny Liston is a jail bird. . . ."

Bob Considine, who writes about everything from doings in the Kremlin to the inside feelings of ballplayer's thighs on slides into second base, said:

"Mel Durslag [*Los Angeles Herald-Examiner* sports columnist] reports that the promoters of the Patterson-Liston fight have requested an Internal Revenue Service ruling on their plan to put $1,700,000 in the deep freeze as the champion's share of what will be a colossal closed circuit TV gate. He would pay taxes (less varied deductions) on a mythical $100,000 a year income over the next 17 years, but not touch the nest egg or draw against it. It would balloon with interest over the years and, at age 44, the one-time juvenile delinquent (Patterson) would receive the whole bundle.

"If Patterson is forced to accept the TV money immediately (he gets 55 percent of the gross sale of an estimated 1,350,000 seats), the man with the whiskers will clobber him for about 90 cents out of every buck.

"A dilemma, to be sure, but one which almost any other man in the land would be happy to shoulder."

Ike Bernstein, an eighty-six-year-old Chicago fight manager, went down to Aurora Downs to see Sonny Liston work out, and, later, had this to say:

"My, what tremendous hands this fellow has! My hand felt like a little boy's in his. There must be an awful lot of power in his fists.

"I'd say he reminds me of Jack Johnson, who, in my book, was the greatest of all heavyweight champions. Sonny is as big as Johnson was, has the same long reach, and can punch.

"He also can box well for a big man, not as well as Johnson, perhaps, but good enough."

There was a "falling out" between Championship Sports, Inc., and the managers of both camps . . . so it was said.

Al Bolan put it into words.

"As to Nilon and D'Amato feeling that Championship Sports, Inc., is falling down on the job," he said, "I've heard that talk before.

"And both will have a tough time convincing their fighters that their (the managers') personal whims are as important as the gross. I have found that with fighters that money talks—just as it does in any other business."

Bolan leveled a vicious blast at Nilon:

"It is quite obvious that (he) is a neophyte in the boxing business. He's a little fish swimming around in a big pond."

One of the big complaints against the promoters was that they were seldom seen at the training camps.

"I have seen both work out and I enjoy it," Bolan said. "But I can't promote and enjoy myself at the same time . . ."

Jimmy Braddock, the heavyweight champion Joe Louis dethroned, picked Patterson to win because Floyd was, in his opinion, "too quick, too wary and a better puncher than rated" while Liston was, according to him, "a one-styled fighter."

Liston spoke up:

"About me being hypnotized, that's bunk. But that Patterson, now, one of his trainers is really a psychiatrist!"

On a particular day, an observer at a workout said to Sonny, "Tell us about today's work."

"I worked," Sonny said.

"Did you feel it was an especially good work, or poor, or average?"

"Average work."

"I thought it was a hell of a work."

"Thank you."

Ye, gads!

The next build-up beef flared over boxing gloves.

There was a "stormy dispute" over the gloves Liston and Patterson would wear into the ring on the night of September 25.

Liston wanted gloves tailored to fit his fourteen-inch fists . . . to be manufactured by the Sammy Frager Company of Chicago.

Patterson's men wanted Everlast gloves . . . made in New York.

So hot was the gloves debate that the fact that Liston's camp had been robbed of three thousand dollars hardly made news.

During the debate, Nilon said to Triner:

"We told you ten days ago that we wanted to use Frager."

"I don't want Frager gloves in the fight, period," said Patterson's man, Dan Florio.

Triner said, "The Commission rules that Liston can use the gloves made for him and Patterson can use the gloves he's chosen. After all, they're both eight-ounce gloves."

Patterson's camp howled a protest.

"In every fight I've heard of," D'Amato said, "the fighters used gloves made by the same company. It's always been done that way and you'd be setting a precedent, believe me."

Triner said the Commission would take the matter under advisement.

In the end, of course, it really didn't matter.

The fighters retired from this beef to a medical examination and were pronounced fit, healthy, alive, with—presumably—twenty-twenty vision. You never know about these things; once a West Coast commission certified a fighter with one glass eye as possessing twenty-twenty vision in both eyes!

Julian Black, former co-manager of Joe Louis with Roxborough, watched a Liston workout and said:

"If this fellow (Patterson) doesn't go right out and take charge, show Liston's who's boss, hurt him, he'll be in trouble. I don't agree with those who think that the longer the fight goes the better for

186

Patterson. The longer it goes the more chance Liston has of catching him."

It was during this workout that a Patterson sparring partner, Ray Lopez of Cuba, swatted Floyd on the jaw with a left. . . .

On September 15, Liston sparred three rounds with Foneda Cox and shadow-boxed two rounds with Aaron Thomas and declared that he was so close to condition for the fight that he was ending his ring work.

Among those impressed by what they saw was Joe Robichaux, a member of the Illinois State Athletic Commission, who said:

"I'm impressed by Liston. He's got weak sparmates? Young Jack Johnson, who is in Patterson's camp, used to spar with Liston, but left because he couldn't take Liston's punches."

Julian Black made a comparison between Liston and Louis:

"Louis used to jar an opponent with one hand and knock him out with the other, but Liston can flatten you with either hand. If he only hits you on the pants, it hurts."

Liston had a few words:

"As things stand now (nine days before the fight), everybody thinks only bad of me. But when I win the championship, then people will see that there's good and bad in everyone."

How important was this fight?

"Winning this title is as important to me as Martin Luther King's fight is for what he's fighting for. I guess that means a lot to all of us."

"What does all this mean to you, Sonny?" Milton Gross asked. "If you become the heavyweight champion, what would you like to do with your life?"

"To show the people how wrong they can be about a person."

"What do you think about now that the fight is getting so close?"

"Nothing. I don't think about nothing."

"What do you think Patterson does best?"

"I never looked at what he does best . . . I guess getting a big pay day. That's what he does best."

There was this conversation:

"Patterson believes he can hit harder than you and take your punch."

"Every man is entitled to his belief. You can't take that away from him. The only way belief can be taken away is the night of the fight."

So spoke Sonny Liston, philosopher.

Sonny had more to say, of tremendous interest, too: "I jab to hurt. That's all. I don't believe in waiting until I get into trouble. I fight to keep out of trouble and I fight to get out of trouble. I fight my own fight. I always fight my own fight. It doesn't matter to me what the crowd is like, whether they're for me or not for me. I don't pay attention to the crowd. I just go in and fight my fight. It doesn't matter who I ever fought. I felt he made just one mistake. I felt his only mistake was getting in the ring with me. The worst person in the world to fight is a scary person."

Tony Weitzel, *Chicago Daily News* columnist, visited Aurora Downs "to see what makes Charles Sonny Liston tick." Weitzel discovered that . . . "as we talked, I began to understand Liston. I even began to like him. Long years ago, I worked with men like Liston on labor gangs, men doomed by race and lack of opportunity to living by their muscles.

"Most of the time, Liston's face is impassive, his eyes veiled. But when he opens up, he has a lusty peasant wit, and a stubborn logic, rigid as a steel bar. Most of his life, you can see, he hasn't relied much on words. Too often, in towns like St. Louis, words can get a black man in trouble. But he observes. He thinks. He works out angles for himself.

"Above all, he feels. Like all his race, Sonny is tremendously and explosively emotional. Like most of his race, he keeps it in, this emotion, when he's in the white folks' world. Now and then, under terrible stress, it has broken out. And when Sonny Liston busts out, it must be like a boiler explosion on a steamboat."

A week before the fight, "secrecy" set into the two training camps. The opponents retreated behind closed doors, to hone up their art for the final tiffing.

"We decided to work on a few things in private," Willie Reddish announced. "We would rather not have any distractions because the things are very important and require complete concentration."

After Liston knocked out Patterson to win the heavyweight title, Sonny gave President John F. Kennedy considerable credit for having forced the issue his way.

In that context, a statement Patterson made to David Condon, the *Chicago Tribune* columnist, begs retelling. The statement, made seven days before the fight, out of Patterson's recollection of his visit with the President.

"This was the greatest thing," Patterson said. "Remember, in the old, 10-cent movies, when we saw the White House? But whoever expected to be inside, let alone talking to the President? Then, there I was. Kennedy tapped my shoulder and said that when others left I should stay. Suddenly, we were real alone.

"I've never been so alone. Even in a fight. Never so scared. Not even when we had real bad trouble with an airplane engine in 1955. If President Kennedy had said, 'Boo!', I would have fainted. I still don't know what he asked me. I just kept saying, 'Yes, yes, yes, yes.'"

Despite the "secrecy" of what was going on behind the closed doors of the two camps, news continued to "leak" out. There was, for example, the little detail of Sonny's skipping rope to a tune called *Lonesome Pine* with a combination of the twist and belly-dance thrown in for good measure.

Explaining that one, Reddish said:

"It's to improve his foot-work . . . we'll be humming the tune from now until fight time and probably even during the fight. We want the tempo to be soaked up by Liston, letting it get to his feet. He takes naturally to the beat of rock 'n' roll stuff."

All this time, of course, the facts and presumptions and rumors and fantasies about Liston's police record was being bandied about the build-up mills. But there were people to be found, if anybody wanted to find them, who had many nice things to say about Sonny. They were to be found, more than a dozen of them, in Sonny's camp.

"Nobody knows what a nice guy he is," said Joe Polino, assistant trainer and cut man. "When things were going slow for me, Liston gave me money, helped me pay the rent. . . ."

Ray Muntzie, Sonny's personal secretary, asked: "What do they want from him? Life is life. When he was in trouble, nobody was around. Now, he's here—everybody's around asking about it. It's hard for him. Most naturally, he has a chip on his shoulder."

Granted that Polino and Muntzie were, like the others, paid "hands." But did they all have to be so unanimous—if they were creators of fiction?

During the numerous interviews, Liston often revealed inner depths, depths of thought and humanity, that surprised his auditors, those who came believing him to be an ignoramus, or close to it.

On the subject of charity, he said: "Favors aren't special; you do them from the way you feel in your heart and you don't tell about them. You do a friend a favor, you don't brag. You don't tell."

On the subject of man's-attitude-toward-man, he said: "Don't be jealous of the other man. If he does better than you, okay, don't be jealous. More power to him."

He also said, "It's wrong to judge a man by what (you) read because sometimes the biggest part is not true . . . people should not judge a man until they know him personally themselves."

As the final pre-fight weekend began, little that was new or significant developed, although a great deal was said and, if possible, much more than that was written. The national interest in a prize fight is a phenomenon of sports. Despite all the anti-Liston talk, the writers and the public both were captivated by the immensity and power and stamina and toughness of this man. Publicity wise, the "rhubarb" over gloves was about the biggest thing anyone had to offer, and chances that this would stop the fight were, of course, nil. Cus D'Amato functioned well as Patterson's publicist—publicist, perhaps, without portfolio, but a skilled talker and creator of "ink" nevertheless. Just as Patterson was more readily talkative than Liston, so was D'Amato more apt to launch off a lengthy treatise than was Jack Nilon, Sonny's adviser. Liston, himself, pressed by interviewers had little to say that was new—for, indeed, as it turned out, he'd said all that needed to be said already. How come everybody thought Patterson was so fast? "Who has he hit so many times in a few moments that you could call him fast?" He was going to win the fight. It wasn't going more than five rounds. Things like that, all said before in one form or another, Liston continued to say. But, he had variations on the old theme. For example, when he was asked on September 21 how long the fight would last, he said: "If it's a cold night, not too long."

Joe Louis thought Sonny was the hardest worker he'd ever seen. Like Sonny, he didn't give speed too much credit. As Louis saw it, Sonny possessed the best left jab in the business and was as strong and powerful as Rocky Marciano. "A lot depends on whether Patterson can hold his temper until they get into the ring," said Joe. "He's getting so mad over what Liston's been saying about him, he might try to fight Sonny at the weigh in."

Sonny closed out his training with a series of workouts that convinced most of the objective observers that Floyd Patterson didn't have a chance. Barney Ross expressed the fear that Floyd would be too proud to run and that, by not running, might well get himself killed. Featured in the last big camp workout was the bit in which Reddish took a stance seven or eight feet away from Liston, then slammed the twelve-pound medicine ball into Sonny's midriff twenty-five times—without any flinching from Sonny, who then did seventy-five sit-ups on a slanted board. All he planned to do after that was jog a couple of miles . . . on Monday, September 24, the day before the fight.

"I think this will be the making of Liston. As champion, his need for battling everybody will have disappeared. He'll rise to be a good champion, the way people rise to being president."
—Cus D'Amato.

CHAPTER XVII

THIS IS HOW SONNY LISTON WON THE WORLD'S HEAVYWEIGHT CHAMPIONSHIP FROM FLOYD PATTERSON ON SEPTEMBER 25, 1962

During his period of reorientation, Sonny Liston is seen with
Father Murphy, Policeman C.J. Stribling.

Sonny says grace before breakfast
as Mrs. Liston serves meal.

At home, Liston is quietly attentive.
Wife is great influence in life.

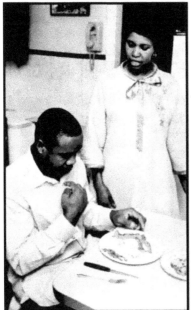

In Forrest City, Ark.,
Mrs. Helen Liston
admires photo of her
son, Sonny, after he has
become the world's
heavyweight champion.

Rare family scene shows
Liston embracing wife
and mother-in-law, Mr.
Eva Crawford, during
visit to St. Louis in
1962.

Liston is all business when training. Here he punches the heavy bag.

Strength of Liston's neck is vividly described by this headstand.

Climax of training camp routine is exercise with the medicine ball, which Sonny catches in midriff without batting an eye.

Liston sharpens speed of hands on the speed-bag.

Sonny skips rope to the
tune of Night Train.

Liston pauses during training
session to sip cup of tea.

Patterson covers up, Liston immediately readies himself for next punch.

Liston's next punch is a left hook—which he cocks for firing.

Patterson is hit and begins plunge towards the ring canvas.

Liston stands over fallen Patterson,
who lies flat on canvas, feet in air.

Sikora signals that fight is over.

Liston's handlers rush to his corner to congratulate him on stunning knockout victory.

Happy new champion and his handlers
pose for photographers in ring.

"You can't say a guy's great just from one fight."
—Ingemar Johansson

"Louis was a combination puncher. Marciano needed combinations. Sonny's the greatest one punch fighter I ever seen."
—Willie Reddish

CHAPTER XVIII

How great is Sonny Liston? It would be folly, as former champ Ingemar Johansson has pointed out, to rate a fighter as "great" off one sensational performance. But there is more to an appraisal of Liston than merely his easy, non-sweat, non-bruise workout with Floyd Patterson.

There are to be considered such items as the man's overall record, the competition he's faced, his punch, his defense, his ring generalship; what greatness means in the context of his times and as compared to other eras . . . things like that.

While considering these items, one cannot, on the other hand, be objective and down-grade these facts:

1) When he met Floyd Patterson, Liston proved himself to be vastly the superior man.

2) He was, when he stepped into the ring to fight Patterson, one of the few heavyweight challengers in boxing history to be rated the favorite over the champion.

3) Seldom, if ever before, had a challenger so completely cleaned up all other competition in his division. In other words, while waiting

in the wings for Patterson and D'Amato to accept him, Liston defeated every worthy championship contender there was. Eddie Machen, Zora Folley, Cleveland Williams, contenders Patterson would never face, for one reason or another, all had been beaten by Liston. He had not fought Archie Moore, but Moore was not seriously considered a heavyweight title challenger at the time Liston defeated Patterson, if, indeed, Moore, luckless in this division, was ever a serious contender after Patterson flattened him in 1956.

Johansson was a name to be bandied about, a possible future foe. But Johansson had eliminated himself, or had been eliminated, as a serious challenger when he lost two out of three to Patterson. In the light of what Liston did to Patterson, it did not seem that Johansson had been missed at all.

There loomed on the horizon but one likely competitor for Liston's title. On the morning of September 26, 1962, that man had to be Cassius Marcellus Clay of Louisville, Kentucky, the aptly named "Louisville Lip." But there were few observers, including the Lip's own thinking-man's camp, who believed that Clay was to be ready for such a fighter as Liston inside two years.

"If Clay lasts four rounds with me," Liston said as he moved into his new Chicago home, "I'd be a disgrace to boxing."

What about Liston's equipment, style?

While defeating Patterson—actually, on the occasion he fought Thurlow Wilson at Jeff City—Liston proved that, in one essential, he rated with the greatest fighters of all times. He was, apparently, born with a tremendous left-hand punch, jab and hook. It was generally acknowledged that Liston's left jab was the greatest since Joe Louis, and there are more who will support the affirmative, than the negative, that Louis' left jab was the all timer.

Style-wise, Liston is more or less orthodox.

Like Louis, he stalks his man relentlessly. He has seldom lost his man, once he's gotten him into difficulty. *His ring discipline is exemplary.*

His right hand is less than a classic punch, but certainly it is powerful and destructive, as a sledge hammer can be powerful and destructive, and even if Patterson could see the punches coming, as he claimed, the same can be said for a tank. You can see it coming; what can you do to stop it? That's the question.

In an era when the heavyweight contender may well be a puffed-up light heavyweight, or a halfback-sized heavyweight, Liston is the full-grown man. Possessed of tremendous shoulders, arms, chest, and gigantic fists, he is a fullback-sized fighter, surprisingly fast and agile for his size, and quite probably the strongest man ever to fight in his division.

He can hit and he can take a hit.

He has demonstrated that convincingly.

He has, in most of his fights, demonstrated the "killer instinct," and he has, in certain of his bouts, proven that, once caressed with a sturdy blow, he becomes aroused and even more dangerous than he is normally. Liston is, in some respects, a throw-back to the old days. That is, he is a product of the kind of hard work and struggle that produces the best of all fighters. His heritage is one of strength and power; it is seen in the sturdiness of his mother, Mrs. Helen Liston, who admits that after she left St. Louis, she returned to Arkansas and "made two crops" with the children. His father was a man who eked out an existence as a sharecropper, literally clawing at the dirt of St. Francis County for his bread, what bread there was.

Liston's childhood, his youth, his being forced to forage, as it were, to live, all built up to the kind of strong man that is needed to withstand the toughest blows. The legend of his prison fights, not shown on the current record, but spoken of nonetheless, argues for a titanic ability to take punishment and to deal it out. His hard work record is impressive. The demonstrations of physical fitness he put on during his training for Patterson were out of Superman's reputation. His willingness to train as hard as Marciano ever did is still another factor in the claim that Liston is a great fighter.

Whatever he may lack in finesse, Liston certainly overcomes in toughness, strength, and the delivered power of his punches. Frank Mitchell claims that he has been "afraid" and perhaps he has; he is a human being. But if any fighter fits the label "fearless," then that fighter must be Sonny Liston. What other fighter in history has faced the best professionals of his day, hobnobbed with the toughies from street gangs to "unwise" adult associations, faced guns, thugs, the entire spectrum of the underside of life and come through without an obvious scratch or mark?

If Tony Anderson's explanation of what happened that time Marty Marshall is said to have knocked Liston down, then he is a champion who has never been knocked off his feet as a professional and has been knocked down only once, by the record, in his entire career. In contrast to Patterson—floored by the likes of Rademacher, Harris, Johansson, et al.—Liston is a veritable rock of Gibraltar.

Liston actually is an awesome heavyweight. People watch him fight or work out and they come away amazed —by his strength and stamina, by his speed and agility (his rope-skipping act is second only to Sugar Ray Robinson's, if second to anyone's), his ring-deadly demeanor. His demolition job on Patterson was so thorough, so swift, so complete that the near-nineteen-thousand in-person onlookers were simply shocked, stunned, startled into silence.

Not even Louis could have beaten Liston's time or thoroughness.

Jack Dempsey could not have been more devastating.

"Sonny Liston would have given Joe Louis all the trouble he wanted, in Joe's own prime," one onlooker said. The thinking is that this would have been a titanic brawl. Both men would be cinches to hit each other, if they could meet in the ring. It would have to be, since both were stalkers, a case of an immovable object meeting an irresistible force; it would have been terrific left vs. terrific left, a great right hand (Joe's) vs. a fair right hand, Liston's superior record of staying on his feet vs. Louis' record of being knocked down ever so often with opponents' right hands. It would have been something to see. Yet any such talk, any comparisons out of era, can be no more than speculation.

Liston cannot soon be ranked with a Louis, who defended his title twenty-five times; nor, in that context, with several other heavyweight champions. While Patterson, Louis, and others came into the championship at an early age, Liston made it at age thirty. Still he dominates his division so completely that he may, as he said the day he moved into his Chicago mansion, hold the title ten more years.

Certainly, it seemed after he demolished Patterson that only old age could whip him. Archie Moore has proven that old age is not necessarily a deterrent to championship competition. Jersey Joe Walcott proved the same thing.

The fact is, Liston may well grow in greatness for a considerable period of time, as a result of pride in the title, extra confidence in himself born of the championship, and his own liking for physical fitness. "I've got to get back into the gym," he said in December, 1962, when no fight was yet scheduled for him. "I'm up to 226 pounds. That's what I weighed this morning."

There are, perhaps, only a tenth of the fighters active in America today that were boxing fifty years ago. The peddlers of nostalgia like to think that the old-timers were vastly greater than the moderns. Yet, there are other experts who declare that many of the legendary fighting figures would be rated as "rank amateurs" today. It is also true that the fighters who kept most active in the old days—such as Jack Johnson, Sam McVey, Sam Langford et al.—fought many "no decision" bouts among themselves. The thought is that, by the very nature of his up-bringing, Liston is far better equipped to step back into boxing history and match the old-timers on power and strength than any other current pugilist. Only Marciano, in recent times, has matched the high type of physical conditioning Liston revealed for his Patterson fight; and Liston's condition wasn't as nearly the product of gym work as was Marciano's, though no heavyweight ever capitalized more on sheer condition than Rocky.

It certainly cannot be said that Liston was protected by the careful handling that Marciano and Patterson received from their managers. Patterson's manager, particularly, picked and chose opponents with all the care a 100-year-old grandmother might exercise while walking through a mine field.

As a champion, Marciano batted 1,000. He was undefeated throughout his professional career. Liston comes very close.

In thirty-five bouts, including his title fight, Liston was beaten (decisioned) only once. That loss was, of course, the eight-round decision won by Marty Marshall at Detroit on September 7, 1954, when he broke Liston's jaw.

Liston knocked out twenty-four of his thirty-five opponents, including Patterson at Chicago. He missed knocking out another, Bert Whitehurst, by about three seconds. He was made to "look bad" by only one fighter, the spoiler, Eddie Machen.

Joe Louis, in his first thirty-five bouts, including four exhibitions, registered thirty-one knockouts. But, since 1958, Liston has kayoed seventeen of twenty opponents. Only Bert Whitehurst (who did it twice) and Eddie Machen went the distance with Liston between January 29, 1958, and September 25, 1962.

The man Liston met on September 25, 1962, didn't even get a chance to fight!

*"Sonny, don't you like to talk about boxing?" a writer asked.
"When I met my wife, I didn't talk too much. So why
should I talk to a man?"*
—From an interview.

CHAPTER XIX

As Sonny Liston walked into a training camp press conference one day, he confronted one of his aides:

"Where's the $50 I asked you to hold for me?"

"I don't know what you're talking about," the aide replied.

"In that case," Sonny said threateningly, "it won't be long before you won't be knowing anything."

Sonny then pulled out a gun and fired twice.

The aide collapsed. A spot of red appeared on his shirt.

A British television executive, who had witnessed the incident, fainted dead away.

He didn't know it was all a joke, planned by Sonny for the occasion. The spot of red on the aide's shirt was ketchup. The shots were blanks.

This was Sonny Liston, practical joker, having his fun. And, contrary to all the dire things said about him, Liston is a fun-loving person. "He's playful," Monroe Harrison has said.

Liston possesses a keen sense of humor. Many of his auditors say it this way: "He has a *wonderful* sense of humor."

He may not be a Milton Berle or a Slappy White, but he is quick-on-the-draw with a quip, the comic one liner, a punch-line.

It is the Sonny Liston gift for making people laugh which will, in time, help him overcome the "bad press" he's gotten.

His wit, or humor, is not contrived. It is natural. It is not strange, then, that, prior to his title bout with Patterson, a great deal of it was flavored with bitterness. Liston was irritated by constant references to his police record.

He was disgusted over financial arrangements for the fight.

He had been put through the wringer about getting his chance. The fact is, Patterson had delayed arrangements for the fight partially in order that his biography, *Victory Over Myself*, could be published.

A great deal of Liston's harsher humor was delivered in derision of Patterson. None of it was turned in on himself. But, then, who does this really well, excepting Jack Benny?

There is to be found in Liston's humor a great deal of sound logic or nitty-gritty thinking or, as Jack Saunders said, mother wit.

A considerable portion of it is classic. Doubtlessly, Liston could have held his own with Joe Louis, who said of Billy Conn: "He can run, but he can't hide."

The fact is, as we've seen, Liston enlarged on this theme more than once while attempting to tell followers of the title contenders that Patterson's speed was vastly overrated as far as this particular contest was concerned.

Following are several additional randomly selected examples of Sonny Liston's method wit:

On the afternoon prior to his fight with Albert Westphal, Liston was asked, "How do you feel? You ready?" "I'm ready to fight fast," he replied. "They pays you the same if you gets him in one minute or the whole ten."

When the telephone rings in Sonny's home, he's liable to answer:

"Your dime, but my time. Talk up. I ain't got much!"

At one point of near-desperation, when Liston thought his chance of meeting Patterson was hopeless, he asked a writer:

"If I slap Patterson's brother-in-law, do you think he'll give me the fight?"

"Why would you want to slap him?"

"Maybe I get Patterson so mad he'll want to fight me."

Once when there was a discussion about Sonny's managers, owners, improper associations and whatall, he said:

"I'm my manager's boss. If I don't fight, they don't make any money."

After Liston whipped Patterson, he was asked about Jack Nilon—whether or not Nilon would be paid for his services.

"If he's doing this for nothing," Liston said, "I want to thank him right now."

While he was training at Aurora Downs, a writer observed: "I notice that you are using your left jab a lot. Does that mean anything?"

"Actually," Sonny said, "I'm doing it for the television cameras. They want to show how good my left is. Also, I am showing it off to you fellows because you'll go back and write stories about my left, and that is what Patterson will read. Then, in the fight, he'll be looking for the left jab and I'll knock him out with the right.

You guys help me a lot; the stuff you write is read and believed."

Another time, Sonny said:

"I'm like Louis. I may look slow, but I'm pretty fast for a guy my size. The big difference, actually, is not in the feet, it's in the hands. I have fast hands, like Louis. When I start throwing punches, they're plenty fast. I believe they are too fast for Patterson to duck, which is what he has done in most of his fights."

After Liston demolished Patterson, a late-arriving writer at the post-fight conference wanted Sonny to tell about the series of punches that brought the knockout and demonstrate them.

"This guy," said Sonny, "wants a late, late show."

While training at Aurora, Liston was asked if he missed his favorite chicken fricassee and fresh strawberry pie, two of Mrs. Liston's specialties.

"Training's hard, but not the food," Sonny replied. "I don't get hungry. Keep thinking about the fight."

After New York refused Liston a license to fight Patterson there, he was asked his reaction. He said:

"It kind of upset me. It was an injustice. The people in New York aren't against me, just a few big men. All that money the hotel and restaurant people lost because they won't get the fight . . . maybe if Rockefeller (Governor of New York) had a hotel or restaurant, he wouldn't have said no to me."

While expressing his disgust with reporters who continued to harp on his past difficulties with the law, Liston said:

"Dig, dig, dig. That's all they do. They don't find anything new. Same old stuff. Pretty soon, a man can't fight if he ever got a traffic ticket. It'll be like the what is it?—the civil service. Have to take an exam."

Liston is renowned as a frightening man. But, he has explained:

"I try to look tough because I'm trying to get the scare on the other guy. And the way some of the suckers fight, I guess they are scared."

On golf:

"I've tried that. But it didn't make no sense to me."

His toughest opponent?

"Cleveland Williams. He had me worried in the first round but then I got him worried in the second round and kept him worried until the third round, when I knocked him out."

On one occasion, when Liston was asked how he'd do with Patterson, probably tired of the direct truth, which must have seemed temporarily ineffectual, he tried evasion:

"If I say I'll beat him, I'm bragging. And if I say I won't, I'm lying. So I don't know what to say."

About one of his opponents:

"He quit before I could knock him out. I was hitting him so fast he couldn't get himself together."

On the early days of his professional career:

"I used to sleep for an hour in the dressing room before a fight. They told me the most important thing was rest. I was like a baby learning to walk. You got to have somebody hold you up at first. Now I don't need anybody but the referee—to pull me off somebody."

In reference to the Philadelphia lady who said Liston impersonated a police officer:

"The woman said she thought I looked like a police officer. I can't help it if she thought I looked like God. I'm not God."

While getting another beef about the press off his chest, Liston said:

"Newspapers are just about the worst thing. They can crucify you. In fact, a man can get whipped in a fight, if he listens to what they say."

When he was asked how it felt to be the world's heavyweight champion, Sonny spoke a volume in one word:

"Good!"

"I like Liston. I don't know exactly why. He seemed like he's lonely and he's been very hurt, both by the press and people's reaction to him. I don't care what he's done. I've known a lot of cats like that, a lot of Negroes with records. To me, Liston is a sweet guy."
—James Baldwin.

CHAPTER XX

On a chilly, gray morning in early December, 1962, a huge, green moving van, the company's name lettered on both sides and back in yellow, pulled up to the entrance of a classically designed, red-brick mansion on the South Side of Chicago and waited to be unloaded. Its contents were the fine, period furnishings of Mr. and Mrs. Charles (Sonny) Liston.

They were moving from Philadelphia. Chicago was to be their new home.

Their new home—a twenty-one-room structure owned by jazz musician Ahmad Jamal, now being rented with an option to buy—was in sharp contrast to Sonny Liston's birthplace in St. Francis County, Arkansas. The selection of this home culminated a two-month search for a new place in which to live on the part of the Listons. Shortly after he won the heavyweight title, he was stopped in Philadelphia "for driving too slow." There was no actual booking. But not long thereafter came the news that the Liston's were leaving that city and "police harassment" was given as a reason.

Nothing about police harassment was mentioned by Sonny when he moved into the Chicago home. Instead, he explained, at a noon press conference called "so that everybody can get the story at the same time," he'd always liked Chicago, he'd gotten his first big breaks in boxing there, and the people always had treated him nicely. It wasn't mentioned but Sonny also had a sister and brother living in nearby Gary, Indiana, where his mother, too, had lived eleven years.

Representatives of the press [including one British reporter], radio, and television came out to cover the event. Lots of film footage was shot for later-that-day presentation on television. Reporters asked Sonny numerous questions and, though his new publicity man, Ben Bentley, was hard by his side, Sonny handled himself marvelously well.

Here was the perfect example of what can happen to the lowliest man, not saying Liston ever was the lowliest man, if he has something on the ball and he is given a chance.

There was nothing in Liston's manner of speech to suggest illiteracy; there was nothing in his demeanor to suggest hoodlumism; there was nothing about him that suggested that he was anything less than the "decent, respectable champion" he'd promised to be, if the public gave him a chance.

He was meticulously dressed in a fine-fitting, gray outercoat with velvet collar, a dark suit, black shoes, white shirt, dark tie, and gray hat. His face showed no scar-tissue, none of the markings of a prize-fighter. He could have been a wealthy business executive, moving into an area which once was home to many of Chicago's wealthiest citizens, which is now home to many of the city's leading Negroes and the Caucasians who refused to run scared when the neighborhood "changed."

Moving into this mansion, which probably would cost $250,000 or more to duplicate today, was not a show off stunt on the part of the Listons.

Originally, they'd sought "a 10-acre place," on which they wanted to build. They'd searched endlessly without finding what they were looking for—although Mrs. Liston said that was still what they wanted. It had been reported that they were buying on 110th Street, on 89th Street, and elsewhere. But, in the final analysis, it seemed that the Jamal home, available because the musician and his wife had split, was the most easily available place for people who wanted to move fast. Mrs. Liston had told me that she preferred a house, even a rental, to an apartment, because she didn't want to place her furniture in an apartment. But, after they took the Jamal house, the Listons admitted that it was too big for the furniture they owned and that half the rooms would probably go unfurnished for a while.

The press conference was held in the huge living room with its stone fireplace and ice-blue drapes and wall-to-wall carpeting. Jamal, being a musician, had installed a house-wide hi-fi system and Sonny, who likes music (Dave Brubeck is his favorite, he said), had already taken advantage of this by putting on some jazz records, which played quietly, insofar as conversation was concerned.

The photographers put Mr. and Mrs. Liston through the paces. Sonny was pictured moving furniture, while Mrs. Liston, a pleasant, smiling, attractive woman, supervised. He was asked to put up Christmas decorations which were, miraculously, handy.

A reporter, apparently well-to-do, happened into the luxurious push-button kitchen while Mrs. Liston was preparing to boil eggs, and began to discuss with her the intricacies of the kitchen, confessing his problems with a similar installation in his home. Mrs. Liston proved to be an expert. All this was nothing new to her. Sonny cooperated pleasantly as he was posed with neighborhood boys on their way home from school (and they were delighted to meet the heavyweight champion). A passing policeman stopped and welcomed Sonny to the city. Passers-by stopped and stared. No one seemed to be less than happy with the new neighbors.

"Which one is Sonny Liston?" asked a well-dressed man.

Sonny Liston was pointed out to him.

"I want to get his autograph," the man said.

During the press conference, the reporters were more interested, actually, in Sonny's fighting plans than they were in the house, though they asked all the necessary questions about the Listons' move to Chicago. Liston said he still intended to give Patterson a match, as their contract specified, but he observed:

"Right now, if I fight Patterson behind that thing we had here, we couldn't fill the basement of this house." Someone wanted to know if he was going to build a gym in the basement.

Sonny said, "No." He said he was going into training, "probably at Coulon's Gym."

Sonny said that he would not fight again under the auspices of Championship Sports, Inc. He had a good reason.

He had not received his full pay-day from Championship Sports, Inc.

He revealed that he had received twenty-five thousand dollars for training expenses and fifty thousand dollars more two weeks after the fight. But the remainder of his purse, more than two hundred and fifty thousand dollars, was tied up in Internal Revenue Service liens on Championship Sports, Inc.

Liston was told that Patterson would like to have their rematch in New York. But Sonny said:

"They didn't want me there when I was the challenger, and I don't know why they'd want me as champion."

He suggested Baltimore as a likelier spot.

Breaking into the fight talk, a reporter wanted to know who had selected the house."

Geraldine (Mrs. Liston) picked it out," said Sonny. "She picks everything."

Liston revealed that his mother-in-law, Mrs. Eva Crawford of St. Louis; and a niece, Margie Wilhite, would live with them in the huge house, as well as Teddy King, his valet; and a sparring partner, Foneda Cox. His first visitor was the Reverend J. A. Potlock, pastor of a nearby church.

Liston said that, after he was settled in Chicago, he wanted to open his own gym, where he would train himself and where, also, he would attempt to influence juvenile delinquents into a better life.

There had been an erroneous story that Sonny was already lined up for a job with a Chicago youth authority. Liston cleared up this report, but said he was certainly interested in any such work. The record was that whenever he had been given an opportunity to talk to juvenile delinquents, he had done a good job. The kids listened as Sonny told them that their delinquency could only lead to trouble, as his own mistakes had brought on many troubles.

Everything about this press conference, this moving into Chicago, suggested that, if Sonny Liston was given a break, he'd do justice to the championship.

Yet, the thought occurred, it was one helluva thing that so many of the people who had opposed his "chance" to fight Patterson, himself a former juvenile delinquent, were now asking so much of Liston, the man they had derided unmercifully.

"What will Sonny Liston do to boxing?" was the title of an article published around the time Sonny moved into his new home.

What could he do to boxing, provided he fought the logical contenders on a fair-and-square basis?

Why, after all these years of horsing around in the game, when not even Federal investigations had resulted in a national czar of boxing, was Sonny Liston expected to clean up a sport that had, almost traditionally, tolerated, if not glorified, wrongdoers? Was the animosity real?

Or was it predicated merely on the fact that Liston hadn't come crawling to the world with a glib confession of sins and an agile plea for forgiveness?

The man had admitted his mistake.

He'd explain how it all happened.

Who can say, for sure, that a man of his background actually knew more than he was telling. Maybe he did. But the annals of boxing are filled with sad stories of fighters who were deluded, deluded and robbed blind, by their so-called benefactors. Or how about Beau Jack, supposedly protected by some smart, honest fellows? Sonny Liston never tried to justify his difficulties, or his mistakes, as being right and moral. He was pitted in investigations against men of college educations and long practice in the art of interrogation. Having been convicted, if not persecuted, he was placed in the precarious position of incriminating himself by people who claimed out loud that he was illiterate.

Nobody shills for crime. That would be stupid. But boxing shills for itself as a rehabilitator.

So a man comes to the point where he can live right and well . . . does one, in a democratic society, continue to whip his head because he was once wrong? Sonny Liston is now a man who can, though he came relatively late to a state of affluence and influence, earn millions with his greatest asset . . . power, stamina, fists.

Is such a man liable to go out and hit some store keeper over the head in a fifty-cent robbery?

Very unlikely.

"Be a champ, act a champ," Sonny said once. "Give me a chance," he said another time, in effect, "and I'll show you I can do all right."

There was evidence, when Sonny moved to Chicago, that he was going to do all right.

He spoke thoughtfully.

He let no one ramrod him into a reply to a question. He evaded no question.

He asked no special favor.

He did not seem ill-at-ease in his new surroundings. He seemed to be a man who was, if later than most, still growing up fast into the admired ways of life.

He went from his new home to Las Vegas, where, on the night Emile Griffith defended his title, he was called to the ring for the benefit of the in-person audience and the television audience.

He was cheered.

Not as loudly as Joe Louis, perhaps.

But cheered, nevertheless.

And he hadn't even defended his title once yet.

APPENDIX

SONNY LISTON: VITAL STATISTICS

Born: 1932, some discrepancy as to actual date
Weight: 214 pounds (weight for Patterson bout in Chicago)
Height: 6 feet, 1 inch
Reach: 84 inches
Neck: 17½ inches
Chest: 44 inches (normal)
Chest: 46½ inches (expanded)
Waist: 33 inches
Biceps: 16½ inches
Fist: 14 inches
Wrist: 8½ inches
Thigh: 25½ inches
Calf: 16 inches
Ankle: 12 inches

SONNY LISTON'S FIGHTING RECORD

— Sept. 2, 1953: Kayoed Doug Smith in first round at St. Louis.
— Sept. 17, 1953: Decisioned Ponce DeLeon in fourth round at St. Louis.
— Nov. 21, 1953: Decisioned Benny Thomas in sixth round at St. Louis.

Summary for 1953: Three fights, three victories.

— Jan. 25, 1954: Kayoed Martin Lee in sixth round at St. Louis.
— Mar. 31, 1954: Decisioned Stan Howlett in sixth round at St. Louis.
— June 29, 1954: Decisioned John Summerlin in eighth round at Detroit.
— Aug. 10, 1954: Decisioned John Summerlin in eighth round at Detroit.
— Sept. 7, 1954: Lost to Marty Marshall in eighth round at Detroit.

Summary for 1954: Five fights, four victories, one lost.

— Mar. 1, 1955: Decisioned Neil Welch in eighth round at St. Louis.
— Apr. 21, 1955: Kayoed Marty Marshall in sixth round at St. Louis.
— May 5, 1955: Kayoed Emil Brtko in fifth round at Pittsburgh.
— May 25, 1955: Kayoed Calvin Butler in second round at St. Louis.
— Sept. 13, 1955: Kayoed Johnny Gray in sixth round at Indianapolis.
— Dec. 13, 1955: Kayoed Larry Watson in fourth round at East St. Louis.

Summary for 1955: Six fights, six victories.

— Mar. 6, 1956: Decisioned Marty Marshall in tenth round at Pittsburgh.

Summary for 1956: One fight, one victory.

1957: Liston was inactive entire year.

— Jan. 29, 1958: Kayoed Bill Hunter in second round at Chicago.
— Mar. 11, 1958: Kayoed Ben Wise in fourth round at Chicago.
— Apr. 3, 1958: Decisioned Bert Whitehurst in tenth round at St. Louis.
— May 14, 1958: Kayoed Julio Mederos in third round at Chicago.
— Aug. 6, 1958: Kayoed Wayne Bethea in first round at Chicago.
— Oct. 7, 1958: Kayoed Frankie Daniels in first round at Miami Beach.
— Oct. 24, 1958: Decisioned Bert Whitehurst in tenth round at St. Louis.
— Nov. 18, 1958: Kayoed Ernie Cab in eighth round at Miami Beach.

Summary for 1958: Eight fights, eight victories.

— Feb. 18, 1959: Kayoed Mike DeJohn in sixth round at Miami Beach.
— Apr. 15, 1959: Kayoed Cleveland Williams in third round at Miami Beach.

— Aug. 5, 1959: Kayoed Nino Valdes in third round at Chicago.

— Dec. 9, 1959: Kayoed Willi Besmanoff in seventh round at Cleveland.

Summary for 1959: Four fights, four victories.

— Feb. 23, 1960: Kayoed Howard King in eighth round at Miami Beach.

— Mar. 21, 1960: Kayoed Cleveland Williams in second round at Houston.

— Apr. 25, 1960: Kayoed Roy Harris in first round at Houston.

— July 18, 1960: Kayoed Zora Folley in third round at Denver.

— Sept. 7, 1960: Decisioned Eddie Machen in twelfth round at Seattle.

Summary for 1960: Five fights, five victories.

— Mar. 8, 1961: Kayoed Howard King in third round at Miami Beach.

— Dec. 4, 1961: Kayoed Albert Westphal in first round at Philadelphia.

Summary for 1961: Two fights, two victories.

Sept. 25, 1962: Kayoed Floyd Patterson in 2:06 of first round to win world's heavyweight championship at Comiskey Park, Chicago.

CAREER SUMMARY: 35 fights, 34 victories, 1 loss (24 knockouts).